Cranial Nerves of the Coelacanth, *Latimeria chalumnae* [Osteichthyes: Sarcopterygii: Actinistia], and Comparisons with other Craniata

Cranial Nerves of the Coelacanth, *Latimeria chalumnae* [Osteichthyes: Sarcopterygii: Actinistia], and Comparisons with other Craniata

R. Glenn Northcutt
Neurobiology Unit,
Scripps Institution of Oceanography,
and Department of Neurosciences,
0201 School of Medicine,
University of California, San Diego,
La Jolla, CA 92093 (USA)

William E. Bemis
Department of Zoology,
University of Massachusetts,
Amherst, MA 01003,
and Department of Ichthyology,
American Museum of Natural History,
New York, NY 10024 (USA)

22 figures (2 in color), 2 tables, 1993

KARGER

Reprint of **Brain, Behavior and Evolution,** Vol. 42, Suppl. 1, 1993

S. Karger
Medical and Scientific Publishers
Basel · Freiburg · Paris · London
New York · New Delhi · Bangkok
Singapore · Tokyo · Sydney

Drug Dosage
The authors and the publisher have exerted every effort to
ensure that drug selection and dosage set forth in this text
are in accord with current recommendations and practice
at the time of publication. However, in view of ongoing
research, changes in government regulations, and the con-
stant flow of information relating to drug therapy and drug
reactions, the reader is urged to check the package insert
for each drug for any change in indications and dosage and
for added warnings and precautions. This is particularly
important when the recommended agent is a new and/or
infrequently employed drug.

© Copyright 1993 by S. Karger AG,
P.O. Box, CH–4009 Basel (Switzerland)
Printed in Switzerland on acid-free paper by
Reinhardt Druck, Basel
ISBN 3–8055–5802–3

Contents

Preface

The living coelacanth, *Latimeria chalumnae*, has fascinated vertebrate biologists for more than 50 years. Surely some interest stems from the famous stories of its discovery and the subsequent search for specimens. After the collection of many specimens from the Comoran archipelago in the 1950s and 1960s, *Latimeria* was the featured subject of beautiful anatomical monographs and frequent symposia. Even now, however, it remains extremely difficult to study living individuals in nature, and there is much to learn about the basic biology of coelacanths.

It is the phylogenetic importance of coelacanths that gives such a storied animal great scientific substance. Following the initial discovery of *Latimeria*, ichthyologists hoped that studies of its biology might reveal much about the ancestry of land vertebrates. This did not happen, at least not in the way originally envisioned. Instead, *Latimeria* fueled debates about the higher phylogenetic relationships of fishes and tetrapods, prompting a search for new characters and new character systems for improved phylogenetic analyses. *Latimeria* was central to several extended phylogenetic debates, and it became important far beyond questions about the origin of tetrapods because it stimulated general interest in phylogenetic research.

This study describes the cranial nerves of a serially sectioned prenatal pup of *Latimeria*. In addition to providing a more detailed account of the nerves than was possible in earlier dissection-based studies, we sought to explore the value of cranial nerves as characters for studying higher relationships within craniates. At the turn of the 20th century, a group of American neuroanatomists including Edward Phelps Allis, Charles Judson Herrick, John Black Johnston, and Harry Waldo Norris described the cranial nerves of several phylogenetically important fishes, yet few modern studies of the higher relationships of craniates even mention any characters of the cranial nerves. We could not say in advance whether such omissions mean that useful characters do not exist or that the characters are difficult to study in a comparative framework. To address this, we defined and surveyed thirty-eight characters of the cranial nerves in a diversity of representative craniates. Most of our characters are shared at the level of Myopterygii (lampreys + gnathostomes), but there are several phylogenetically interesting characters which demonstrate the promise of this character system for future phylogenetic research.

We were able to start and complete this project thanks to Gareth Nelson, who allowed us extended access to the sectioned prenatal pup of *Latimeria* at the American Museum of Natural History. Micro Video Instruments (Avon, Massachusetts) loaned equipment essential for our study. Special thanks to Jane Bemis for translations, and to Judith Shardo and Sue Commerford for assistance in preparing the manuscript. Eric Findeis, Preston Holmes and Roy Doyon aided with figures, and we are grateful to Larry Schwartz for extended access to his Macintosh. Robert L. Boord criticized the manuscript. Support for our studies of coelacanths was provided by Jane H. Bemis, the Donn Rosen Fund, and the Tontogany Creek Fund. Additional support during the period of research was provided by grants from the Whitehall Foundation, NSF (BSR-8806539, BSR-9119561 and a special monographic supplement BSR-9220938), and NIH (NS24669 and NS24689). Finally, this project renewed our respect for the achievements of the early comparative neuroanatomists. Many thanks to them and to our patient spouses, Mary Sue Northcutt and Betty McGuire.

R. Glenn Northcutt and
William E. Bemis
Scripps Institution of Oceanography, March, 1993

Abbreviations

I	olfactory nerve	b5	ramule 5 of buccal ramus of anterodorsal lateral line nerve
II	optic nerve	bas	basisphenoid
III	oculomotor nerve	bcm	basicranial muscle
IV	trochlear nerve	buc	buccal ramus of anterodorsal lateral line nerve
VI	abducent nerve	buc+max	buccal+maxillary complex=buccal ramus of anterodorsal lateral line nerve and maxillary ramus of trigeminal nerve
VII	facial nerve		
VIII	octaval nerve		
IX	glossopharyngeal root		
1p X	first pharyngeal ramus of vagal nerve	c	corpus of the cerebellum
1pr X	first pretrematic ramus of vagal nerve	cb1	ceratobranchial 1 (bone or cartilage)
1pt X	first posttrematic ramus of vagal nerve	cb2	ceratobranchial 2 (bone or cartilage)
2p X	second pharyngeal ramus of vagal nerve	cb3	ceratobranchial 3 (bone or cartilage)
2pr X	second pretrematic ramus of vagal nerve	cb4	ceratobranchial 4 (bone or cartilage)
3br	third branchial trunk of vagal nerve	cb5	ceratobranchial 5 (bone or cartilage)
a	cerebellar auricle	cc	communicating canal
a O	anterior ramus of otic lateral line nerve	cer	ceratohyal (bone or cartilage)
a pro	anterior process of prootic (cartilage)	cg	ciliary ganglion
a ST	anterior ramus of supratemporal lateral line nerve	chg	choroidal gland innervated by ciliary 'nerve'
ac	most anterior contact of abducent nerve with basicranial muscle	cm	coracomandibular muscle
		cn III	ventral ramule of dorsal ramus of oculomotor nerve carrying fibers of the ciliary ganglion
AD	anterodorsal lateral line nerve		
adm	mandibular adductor muscle	cr	sensory crypts of olfactory epithelium
aec	anterior ethmoid commissure	cson	posterior canal for supraorbital ramus in sphenethmoid cartilage
af	afferent branchial artery		
ahm	hyomandibular adductor muscle	d	dorsal ramus of posterior lateral line nerve
an	anterior naris	d ST	dorsal ramus of supratemporal lateral line nerve
ao	antotic process of ethmosphenoid	d-man	dorsal ramule of trigeminal mandibular ramus
ar	anterior ramule of superficial ophthalmic ramus of anterodorsal lateral line nerve (=so2)	di	diencephalon
		dlf	dorsal lip fold
art	anterior rostral tube	dm	dorsal ramule of mandibular ramus of facial nerve
ascc	anterior semicircular canal	dr	dorsal root of anterodorsal lateral line nerve
AV	anteroventral lateral line nerve	dr III	dorsal ramus of oculomotor nerve to superior rectus muscle
b AV?	possible buccal ramus of anteroventral lateral line nerve		
		dr IX	dorsal ramule of posttrematic ramus of glossopharyngeal nerve (=posttrematic internus of Norris [1925b])
b1	ramule 1 of buccal ramus of anterodorsal lateral line nerve		
b2	ramule 2 of buccal ramus of anterodorsal lateral line nerve	dr X	dorsal ramule of first posttrematic ramus of vagal nerve
b3	ramule 3 of buccal ramus of anterodorsal lateral line nerve	ds	dorsal root of spinal nerve
		eb1	epibranchial 1 (bone or cartilage)
b4	ramule 4 of buccal ramus of anterodorsal lateral line nerve	eb2	epibranchial 2 (bone or cartilage)
		eb3	epibranchial 3 (bone or cartilage)

ef	efferent branchial artery
elm 1	element of ventral ramule of posttrematic ramus of glossopharyngeal nerve innervating levator muscle of glossopharyngeal arch
end	endolymphatic duct
eph	epihyal (bone or cartilage)
et	ethmosphenoid portion of braincase
ex	extrinsic eye muscles innervated by oculomotor nerve
g AD	ganglion of anterodorsal lateral line nerve
g AV+VII	ganglia of anteroventral lateral line and facial nerves
g MLLN	ganglion of middle lateral line nerve
g O	ganglion of otic lateral line nerve
g PLLN	ganglion of posterior lateral line nerve
g Pr	ganglion of profundal nerve
g ST	ganglion of supratemporal lateral line nerve
g V	sensory ganglion of trigeminal nerve
g Vmot	motor fibers passing through ganglion of trigeminal nerve
g Vsom	sensory somata in ganglion of trigeminal nerve
gh	geniohyoid muscle
gp	fascicles of ventral ramule of posttrematic ramus of glossopharyngeal nerve+first pretrematic ramus of vagal nerve
gup	gular plate
h	hypophysis or hypophyseal vessels
hhb	hyoid hemibranch
hscc	horizontal semicircular canal
hy	hyoid ramus of facial nerve
hym	hyomandibular trunk of the facial nerve
hyo	hyomandibula (bone or cartilage)
ica	internal carotid artery
ie	inner ear
im	intermandibular muscle, anterior portion
imp	intermandibular muscle, posterior portion
in	intrinsic eye muscle innervated by ciliary 'nerve'
ioc	infraorbital sensory canal
iom	inferior oblique muscle
iom III	ramule of oculomotor nerve to inferior oblique muscle
irm	inferior rectus muscle
irm III	ramule of oculomotor nerve to inferior rectus muscle
ivs	portion of intracranial venous sinus
jv	jugular vein
l PLLN	lateral ramus of posterior lateral line nerve
l1p X	lateral ramule of first pharyngeal ramus of vagal nerve
lcr	long ciliary ramus
ld	lateral division of the lateral element of the ventral ramule of the posttrematic ramus of the glossopharyngeal nerve
ldd	lateral division of the lateral element of the dorsal ramule of the mandibular ramus of the trigeminal nerve
led	lateral element of the dorsal ramule of the mandibular ramus of the trigeminal nerve
lg IX	lateral ganglion of glossopharyngeal nerve
lg X	lateral ganglion of vagal nerve
llf	lateral line canal fenestra
lm	labial muscle
lm1	levator muscle of branchial arch 1

lm2	levator muscle of branchial arch 2
long	long root of ciliary ganglion
lor	ramule of lateral ramule of opercular ramus of facial nerve
lp IX	lateral ramule of pharyngeal ramus of glossopharyngeal nerve
lpal 1	first lateral ramule of palatine ramus of facial nerve
lpal 2	second lateral ramule of palatine ramus of facial nerve
l1pt X	first posttrematic ramus of vagal nerve
lr	lateral ramule of buccal+maxillary ramus
lrm	lateral rectus muscle
lrm III	ramule of oculomotor nerve to lateral rectus muscle
ltc	lateral trunk sensory canal
lw	lateral wall of the olfactory sac
m	medulla oblongata
m AV	mandibular ramus of anteroventral lateral line nerve
m V	mandibular ramus of trigeminal nerve
m VI	medial ramus of VI innervating basicranial muscle
m VII	mandibular ramus of facial nerve
m1p X	medial ramule of first pharyngeal ramus of vagal nerve
m2p X	medial ramule of second pharyngeal ramus of vagal nerve
m4	fourth ramule of mandibular ramus of trigeminal nerve
mac	mandibular canal
max	maxillary ramus of trigeminal nerve
mc	Meckel's cartilage
md	medial division of the lateral element of the ventral ramule of the posttrematic ramus of the glossopharyngeal nerve
mdd	medial division of the lateral element of the dorsal ramule of the mandibular ramus of the trigeminal nerve
me	medial element of the ventral ramule of the posttrematic ramus of the glossopharyngeal nerve
mec	median sensory canal
med	medial element of the dorsal ramule of the mandibular ramus of the trigeminal nerve
mes	mesencephalon
mg IX	medial ganglion of glossopharyngeal nerve
mg X	medial ganglion of vagal nerve
MLLN	middle lateral line nerve
mor	medial ramule of opercular ramus of facial nerve
mp IX	medial ramule of pharyngeal ramus of glossopharyngeal nerve
mpal	medial ramule of palatine ramus of facial nerve
mrm	medial rectus muscle
mr	medial ramule of buccal+maxillary ramus
mr V	motor root of trigeminal nerve
mrm III	ramule of oculomotor nerve to medial rectus muscle
not	notochord
nt	nasal tectum (cartilaginous)
O	otic lateral line nerve
o2	second ramule of posterior ramus of otic lateral line nerve
o3	third ramule of posterior ramus of otic lateral line nerve
ob	olfactory bulb

oc	otic commissure of otic lateral line nerve	r VI	recurrent ramus of abducent nerve supplying basicranial muscle
oe	olfactory epithelium	rap	retroarticular process
on	roots of occipital nerves	rb	rostral body
onv	orbitonasal vein	r IX	sensory and motor roots of glossopharyngeal nerve
op	olfactory peduncle	rm	medial rectus muscle
opc	opercular cartilage	roe	rostral organ epithelium
or	opercular ramus of facial nerve	r Pr	root of profundal nerve
os	olfactory sac	sac	sacculus of inner ear
ot	optic tectum	sboc	subopercular sensory canal
otc	otic sensory canal	sc	sclera of the eye
oto	otolith	scr	short ciliary ramus
ovs	components of orbital venous sinus	short	short root of ciliary ganglion
p	most posterior contact of abducent nerve with basicranial muscle	SM	somatomotor nucleus of oculomotor nerve
		so	superficial ophthalmic ramus of anterodorsal lateral line nerve
p IX	pharyngeal ramus of glossopharyngeal nerve		
p O	posterior ramus of otic lateral line nerve	so 5	the fifth ramule of the superficial ophthalmic ramus
p1	ramule 1 of profundal nerve	soc	supraorbital sensory canal
p2	ramule 2 of profundal nerve (dorsal ciliary 'nerve')	som	superior oblique muscle
p3	ramule 3 of profundal nerve	spc	spiracular chamber
p4	ramule 4 of profundal nerve	sr	spiracular ramule of posterior ramus of otic lateral line nerve
p5	ramule 5 of profundal nerve		
p6	ramule 6 of profundal nerve	srm	superior rectus muscle
p7	ramule 7 of profundal nerve	srm III	dorsal ramule of dorsal ramus of oculomotor nerve supplying the superior rectus muscle
p8	ramule 8 of profundal nerve		
p9	ramule 9 of profundal nerve	srV	sensory root of trigeminal nerve
p10	ramule 10 of profundal nerve	SS	somatosensory projection of profundal nerve
pal	palatine ramus of facial nerve	ST	supratemporal lateral line nerve
pao	antotic process of basisphenoid	stc	supratemporal sensory canal
pb X	posterior branch of the vagal nerve possibly innervating the last three gill arches	sym	symplectic (bone or cartilage)
		t IX	sensory and motor trunk of glossopharyngeal nerve
pb1	pharyngobranchial 1	t V	sensory and motor trunk of trigeminal nerve
pb2	pharyngobranchial 2	t X	sensory and motor trunk of vagal nerve
pc	connecting process of the ethmosphenoid for articulation with prootic	tc	temporal sensory canal
		tel	telencephalic hemisphere
peb2	accessory cartilage anterior to epibranchial 2	ton	tongue
pec	posterior ethmoid commissure	v ST	ventral ramus of supratemporal lateral line nerve
pi	opening of posterior inferior rostral tube	v X	visceral ramus of vagal nerve
pit	posterior inferior rostral tube	v-man	ventral ramule of mandibular ramus of trigeminal nerve
PLLN	posterior lateral line nerve		
pn	posterior naris	vc	ventral ciliary 'nerve'
poc	preopercular sensory canal	vg	fascicles of pretrematic+ventral ramules of posttrematic rami of vagal nerve
pq	palatoquadrate cartilage		
Pr	profundal nerve	ViM(EW)	visceral motor nucleus of ciliary ganglion, Edinger-Westphal nucleus
pr IX	pretrematic ramus of glossopharyngeal nerve		
pro	prootic (bone or cartilage)	ViS	visceral sensory projection of ciliary 'nerve'
ps	opening of posterior superior rostral tube	vlf	ventral lip fold
pscc	posterior semicircular canal	vm	ventral ramule of mandibular ramus of facial nerve
psp	parasphenoid	vr III	ventral ramus of oculomotor nerve to inferior rectus, medial rectus, and inferior oblique muscles
pst	posterior superior rostral tube		
pt IX	posttrematic ramus of glossopharyngeal nerve		
ptc	posttemporal sensory canal	vr IX	ventral ramule of posttrematic ramus of glossopharyngeal nerve
q	quadrate portion of palatoquadrate		
r ML	ramus of middle lateral line nerve	vr V	motor root of trigeminal nerve
r POL	roots of postotic lateral line nerves (=root of middle, supratemporal and posterior lateral line nerves)	vr X	ventral ramule of first posttrematic ramus of vagal nerve
		vs	ventral root of spinal nerve

Introduction

Much is already known about the structure of the brain of the coelacanth, *Latimeria chalumnae* [Smith, 1939a; Lemire, 1971; Northcutt et al., 1978; Kremers and Nieuwenhuys, 1979]. Only a few studies, however, have dealt with the peripheral distribution of the cranial nerves, and most of the information in these studies has been based on dissection of adult specimens [Smith, 1939b; Millot and Anthony, 1958, 1965; Millot et al., 1978]. In dissecting large specimens, critical details of the innervation pattern are likely to be missed. Also, it is generally impossible to accurately assess the structure and relationships of the cranial ganglia based only on dissections. It is important to obtain such information because a detailed understanding of the comparative anatomical relationships of the cranial ganglia is essential for understanding the development and evolution of the cranial nerves.

In this paper, we describe the cranial nerves of a prenatal pup of *Latimeria chalumnae* based on the same series of histological sections studied for a previous paper [Bemis and Northcutt, 1991]. In addition to the possibility of discovering new features of the cranial nerves of *Latimeria*, we had other important reasons for making this study. Recently, there has been considerable progress in understanding the comparative anatomy of the lateral line and branchiomeric nerves of fishes, and since Millot and Anthony [1965] summarized their observations on the cra-

nial nerves of *Latimeria*, there have been many important revisions in interpretation and terminology. We are also interested in relating the patterns of the cranial nerves to cranial segmentation. For example, the basicranial muscle is almost certainly a derivative of a preotic somite [Bemis and Northcutt, 1991; see Northcutt, 1990 and Noden, 1991 for general reviews]. In the present paper, we explore questions about the serial homology of the rami of the branchiomeric nerves. Because of the phylogenetic significance of *Latimeria*, we felt it important to provide an updated reinterpretation of its cranial nerves, and we hope this ultimately will facilitate interpretation of fossil actinistians as well as other fossil and living fishes [Rosen et al., 1981; Lauder and Liem, 1983; Maisey, 1986; Bemis et al., 1987; Musick et al., 1991; Schultze, 1991]. We summarize our phylogenetic information using a character matrix and cladogram, which also helps to indicate where future comparative study of cranial nerves is needed.

The specimen we studied is prenatal. Some ontogenetic changes in the nervous system of *Latimeria* are known (e.g., great allometric lengthening of some rami [Anthony, 1980]), but for present purposes the pup is a miniature adult in which all nerves and innervated tissues are present. Because this material is unique, we have attempted to describe the nerves in detail and to provide extensive illustrations and specific references to the series of sections.

Materials and Methods

The study is based on our serial reconstruction of the head of a single prenatal pup from the collections of the American Museum of Natural History. A detailed account of the original preparation of the histological series and our renumbering of the sections of this specimen was published previously [Bemis and Northcutt, 1991]. Because this information is critical for understanding our reconstruction, most of it is included again for the reader's convenience. The Appendix summarizes the various numbers which have been applied to these slides.

The discovery of prenatal pups of *Latimeria* in a specimen at the American Museum of Natural History was one of the most exciting events in the history of coelacanth research [Smith et al., 1975; Atz, 1976]. The mother is a very large specimen (AMNH 32949; CCC 29) collected off Mutsamudu on Anjouan Island on 7 January 1962 by native fishermen and preserved whole in formalin by G.W. Garrouste. When the specimen was dissected, five pups were discovered (see Wourms et al., 1991 for description of viviparity in *Latimeria*). The first of these pups (AMNH 32949h, 301 mm TL; CCC 29.1) is the specimen prepared histologically and described here. Although a color photograph of this specimen was taken prior to sectioning [Myking, 1977], it is not a directly lateral view, and therefore is unsuitable for determining an outline of the head for a reconstruction in the lateral plane. Fortunately, a lateral view of pup 2 (AMNH 32949, 308 mm TL; CCC 29.2) was available and is adequate for establishing the plane of section for pup 1 (fig. 1), but it could not provide the basis for a lateral reconstruction due to individual variation between the two specimens. For this reason we made a dorsal reconstruction.

Our interpretation of the initial transection of the head of pup 1 is shown in figure 1A (inset). The anterior portion (Block A) includes the snout and eye; the posterior portion (Block B) includes the ear region and all but the most caudal portions of the gill arches; Block C was cut through the cloacal region and was not examined for this study. We estimate that the total original length of Blocks A and B was 58 mm. This estimate was made by comparing the unsectioned trunk of pup 1 with the photograph of pup 2. The two blocks were embedded in nitrocellulose and sectioned at 50 μm in the laboratory of Michael D. Lagios. Fortunately, the blocks were not sectioned in a perfectly transverse plane; there is a slight lateral offset of the right and left sides so that the right side of the specimen extends slightly more caudal than the left side. This right-left offset proved to be especially helpful in reconstructing the otic region.

The sections were stained with Weigert's hematoxylin and Van Gieson's picro-fuchsin and are suitable for detailed study and photomicrography; the preservation of histological detail is surprisingly good. The sections were apparently stained and mounted at two different times. The initial run included every 10th section (more or less), and these sections were mounted individually on large lantern slides (8.3 × 10.2 cm). Sometime later, the intervening sections were stained and mounted on conventional 2″ × 3″ (5 cm × 7.5 cm) slides. In general, these intervening sections are better stained than those of the initial run.

When we received the slides for study, they were in disarray and lacked any preparation notes. We therefore had

Fig. 1. Lateral views of pups of *Latimeria*. **A** Photograph of pup 2 (AMNH 32949, 308 mm TL) with inset drawing to show plane of sectioning and boundaries of Blocks A and B. Apparently no lateral photograph of the sectioned specimen (AMNH 32949h, 301 mm TL) was made before sectioning. Full details about the histological preparation of pup 1 are provided in the text. **B** Diagram of cranial sensory canals of pup based on figure in Hensel [1986] showing our revised terminology for the canals. The openings of the posterior superior (ps) and posterior inferior (pi) rostral tubes are also indicated.

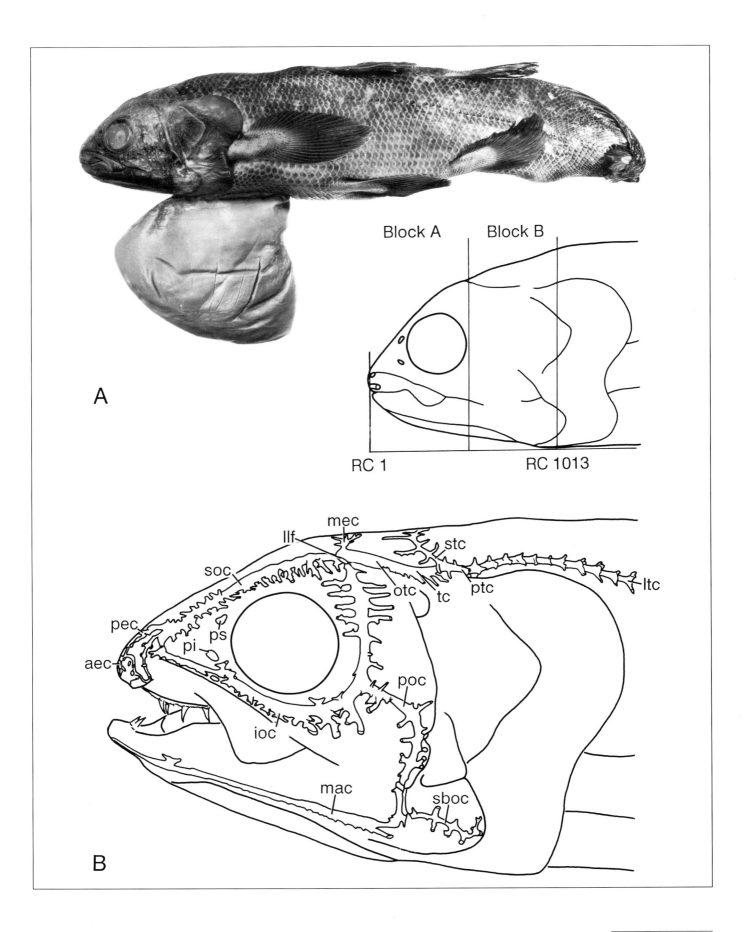

Block A   Block B

RC 1   RC 1013

A

B

mec
llf
stc
soc
otc
tc
ptc
ltc
pec
ps
pi
poc
aec
ioc
mac
sboc

to sort and renumber them before beginning our work. The original numbers recorded on the slides are 'packet numbers'. Block A was cut from the caudal to rostral direction into 550 sections, which, as nitrocellulose sections are typically handled, were put into packets. Packets A1, A2, A3, A4 and A5 originally included 100 sections each, and packet A6 (the most anterior part of the head) had 50 sections. The packet numbers probably were stamped with a numbering machine on papers interleaved between sections; in any event, the packet numbers were separated from the sections prior to mounting and transcribed to typed paper labels affixed to the slides. Despite some mistakes in transcription, the packet numbers of the A series are a good guide to the actual section order; based on these numbers only about 50 sections from Block A are missing from the set.

Block B was also sectioned from the caudal to rostral direction; again, based on the packet numbers, we believe it resulted in about 550 sections. These sections were divided into packets B1, B2, B3, B4, and B5 (each with 100 sections) and a final packet B6 (with 54 sections). The ordering based on packet numbers for the B series is wrong in many cases. Also, an estimated 90 sections were lost from packet B3 in the time between preparation of the lantern slide series and the final preparation of the 2″×3″ slides.

After the sections were mounted, a second series of numbers was apparently assigned to both lantern slides and the 2″×3″ slides in an attempt to provide a consistent rostral to caudal numbering scheme. Unfortunately, because the slides were so badly out of order, this attempt was a failure (Appendix).

Before we began our work, we studied and compared each of the 915 available slides (from what we believe was an original total of 1,104 sections) to determine its actual position in the series. Red flag dots were placed in the lower left hand corner of each slide to allow consistent right-left orientation of the sections (many of the sections were mounted upside down). We then assigned a new set of 'rostral to caudal' (RC) numbers, starting with RC 1 at the tip of the snout. We left a total of 98 blanks to cover loss of sections where we could identify gaps of greater than two sections based on the original packet numbers and careful inspection of the sections; all of these gaps turned out to be in the otic region in the area of packet B3 noted above, and we refer to this area in our text as 'the gap'. Fortunately, the series of lantern slides prepared from every tenth section was available for the otic region, so that the gap did not prevent reconstruction; also, the slight right-left offset due to the plane of section made it possible for us to use infor-mation from both sides of the lantern slides through the otic region. We assumed that any remaining small inconsistencies would work out in the reconstruction itself, and began our work with 1,013 sections present or accounted for.

Throughout the detailed description of the structures, we make reference to our RC numbers. In addition, our RC numbers are keyed to the axes of the reconstructions provided in figures 2 and 3.

We judged that this project could not be handled by the computer assisted reconstruction software then available to us, so we prepared our reconstruction by hand. We reconstructed only the left side of the specimen at 10 times life size, working from a dorsal perspective. This allowed us to use a midsagittal line drawn through the tracing of each section as the line of registration. We projected and traced every 25th section, plotted the nerves and other structures of interest, transferred the tick marks to the master reconstruction, and connected the outlines. Additional tracings of sections and comprehensive notes were needed for the final descriptions.

In addition to the pup, we studied sectioned brains of three other specimens of *Latimeria* to confirm details about the nerve roots. Previous reports on the neuroanatomy of these specimens have been made [Northcutt et al., 1978; Northcutt, 1987] and these specimens are listed in the catalog of coelacanths provided by Bruton and Coutouvidis [1991] as CCC 59 (FMNH 97106), CCC 61 (FMNH 96057), and CCC 80. They were embedded in paraffin, sectioned at 15 μm and stained with either Bodian or Klüver-Barrera methods.

Fig. 2. Main reconstruction of the cranial nerves in dorsal view. The nerves are color coded to show their components: red – motor; blue – lateral line; green – somatic sensory; yellow – visceral sensory. The RC section numbers from 1 to 1,000 are indicated with tick marks on the longitudinal axis. The figure numbers of the eight levels through which sections are shown are indicated. The region of the gap is also shown by a black bar along the axis. **A** Nerves and key sense organs of the dorsal portion of the head. The position of the eye and the lateral outline of the head are shown for reference. Other key landmarks include the rostral organ, which consists of the sensory epithelium (roe) and three tubes that connect with the exterior (anterior rostral tube, art; posterior inferior rostral tube, pit; and the posterior superior rostral tube, pst). An outline of the brain is also shown, including the olfactory peduncle (op), the rostral body (rb), telencephalon (tel), diencephalon (di), optic tectum (ot), cerebellum (c) and medulla (m). All labeled nerves and rami are described in the text. **B** Nerves and key sense organs of the ventral part of the snout, lower jaw, and ventral portions of the gill region. Landmarks include the anterior naris (an), olfactory sac (os), and olfactory epithelium (oe).

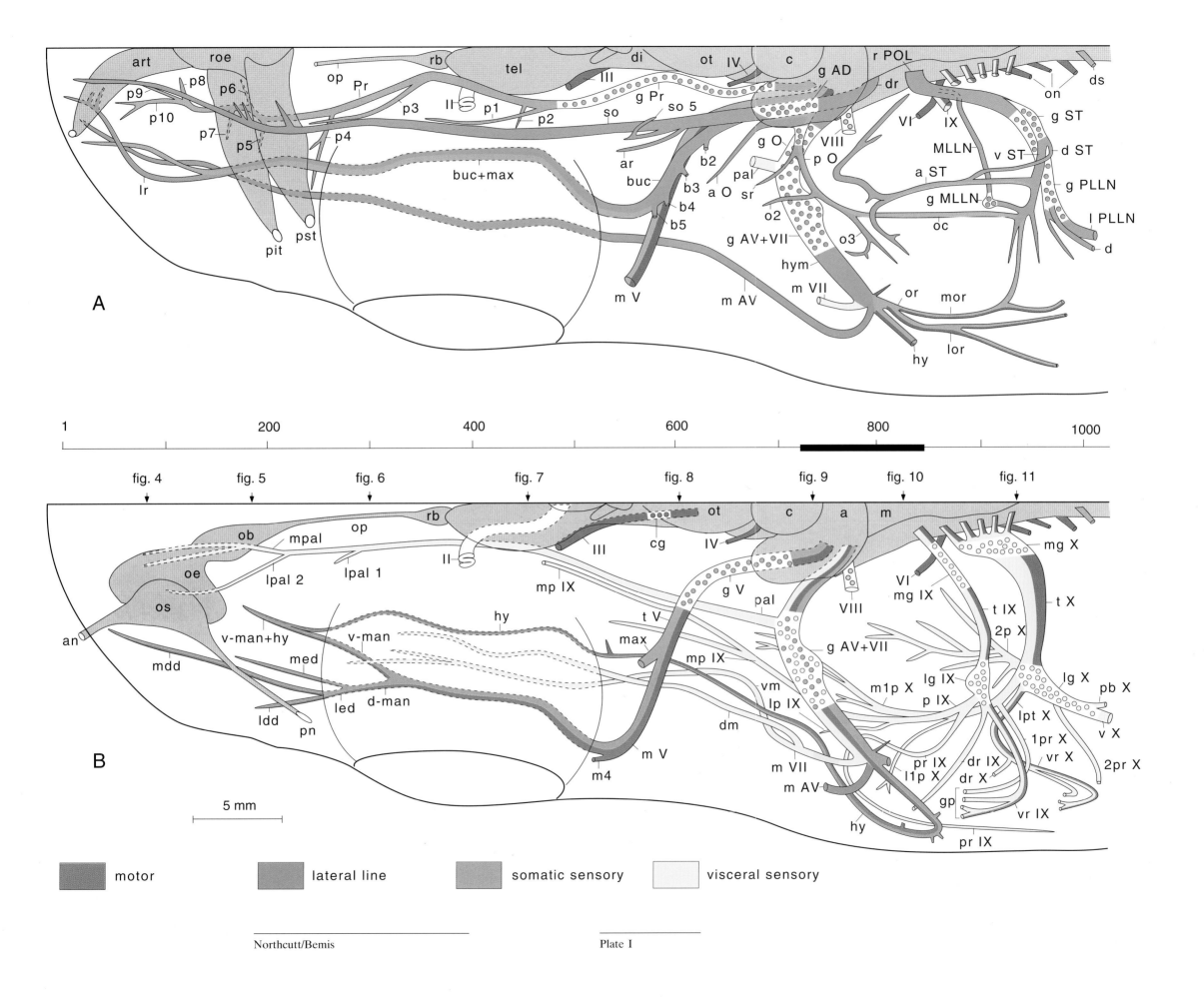

A

| 1 | 200 | 400 | 600 | 800 | 1000 |

fig. 4   fig. 5   fig. 6   fig. 7   fig. 8   fig. 9   fig. 10   fig. 11

B

5 mm

| motor | lateral line | somatic sensory | visceral sensory |

Northcutt/Bemis

Plate I

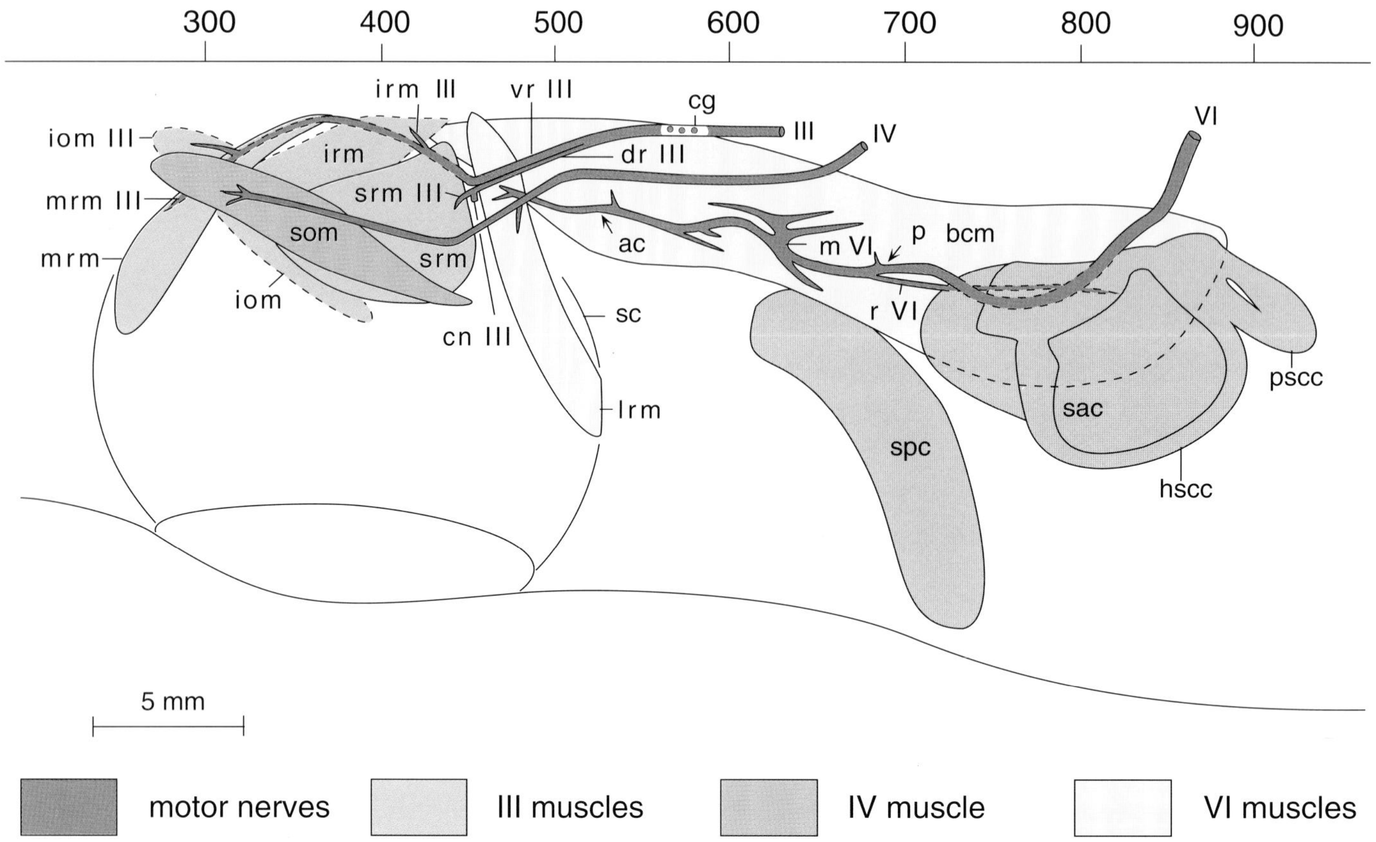

Fig. 3. Extraocular muscles and their nerves. The nerves are indicated in red to indicate their motor function. Positions of the sclera of the eye (sc), the spiracular chamber (spc) and inner ear (ie) are indicated for reference. This reconstruction is printed at a slightly smaller magnification than is figure 2.

Plate II   Northcutt/Bemis

Conventions

In the process of our study, we developed our abbreviations by adopting certain nomenclatural and illustrative conventions.

Cranial nerves usually are described according to this descending hierarchy: trunk, ramus, ramule, element, division, branch. It is not traditional or practical in all cases to adhere strictly to the implications of this hierarchical scheme. For instance, some large rami may be described as giving off several small ramules for neuromasts (e.g., the superficial ophthalmic ramus of the anterodorsal lateral line nerve). In other cases, we describe the divergence of a ramus into two more or less equally sized ramules, even though both ramules may remain relatively large (e.g., d-man and v-man, the dorsal and ventral ramules of the mandibular ramus of the trigeminal nerve, respectively).

Nerves are abbreviated and figured as follows:

1. Abbreviations for nerves start with capital letters or the Roman numeral of the nerve (e.g., Pr is the profundal nerve; III is the oculomotor nerve). These abbreviations are never combined with any modifiers but, if a modifier is needed then it is set off by a space (e.g., p IX is the pharyngeal ramus of the glossopharyngeal nerve).

2. Ganglia are designated by a lower case 'g' before the abbreviation of the nerve (e.g., g Pr).

3. Where there is an obvious anastomosis (such as the fusion of the buccal ramus of the anterodorsal lateral line nerve with the maxillary ramus of the trigeminal nerve) or what we interpret as a phylogenetic combination of structures (such as the fusion of the ganglion of the anteroventral lateral line nerve with the ganglion of the facial nerve), we represent this with a '+' sign (for these two examples, buc+max and g AV+VII, respectively).

4. All rami are named and indicated in the figures, and most ramules discussed in the text are named or numbered and included in the figures.

5. Names of nerves are anglicized (e.g., abducent nerve) except when specific reference is made to a previous study.

Other conventions for coding and labeling the illustrations are as follows:

1. The main reconstruction (fig. 2) is color coded to show nerve components: red, motor; blue, lateral line; green, somatic sensory; and yellow, visceral sensory.

2. In both reconstructions (fig. 2, 3), circles filled with the appropriate color indicate the extent of each ganglion.

3. In both reconstructions where the course of a nerve would be obscured in dorsal view by other structures, the nerve is shown with dashed lines.

4. In the diagrams of eight levels through the specimen (fig. 4–11), light gray indicates cartilages and bones, darker gray indicates muscles, and black indicates nerves.

It was not our intent to document all cranial structures in the pup, but many must be mentioned in describing the courses of the nerves. For cranial bones, muscles and cartilages, we adopted the nomenclature developed by Millot and Anthony [1958, 1965] and Millot et al. [1978]. For the cranial sensory canals we revised Hensel's [1986] nomenclature based on our study of the lateral line canals in the pup and additional adult specimens (fig. 1B).

A black bar on the longitudinal axis of the main reconstruction (RC 732 to RC 839, fig. 2) indicates the 'gap', the region in which only every tenth section was available.

Results

The Results section is divided into ten subsections describing individual nerves or functionally related groups of nerves. For each sensory nerve, we begin with a description of the ganglion, then describe the nerve's root, and last its peripheral distribution. Motor nerves are traced distally from their point of emergence from the brainstem.

Unless stated otherwise, the descriptions are based on the left side of the specimen only. Throughout the text, we refer to the approximate histological section (numbers preceded by an 'RC'); in some cases indicated structures may also appear in adjacent sections.

Figures for the Results section are organized as follows. The main reconstruction (fig. 2) is divided into two parts. The first part (fig. 2A) illustrates the nerves of the rostral organ and dorsal portion of the head; the second part (fig. 2B) includes the olfactory system and the nerves of the lower jaw, gill arches and other ventral structures. Figure 3 is a reconstruction of the eye muscles, the basicranial muscle, and their nerves, with the outlines of the spiracular chamber and ear included for general reference. Figures 4–11 are transverse sections and accompanying line drawings through eight levels of the pup. Figures 12–17 illustrate histological details of the ganglia, nerves and selected sensory organs in rostral to caudal sequence. Figures 18 and 19 summarize relationships of the glossopharyngeal nerve and gill arches.

Olfactory Nerve

The olfactory organ of *Latimeria* is crescent shaped in dorsal view, with a tubular anterior naris and a long slit-like posterior naris (an, os, pn; fig. 2B). The organ is housed in a large cavity in the ethmoid portion of the sphenethmoid cartilage (fig. 4). The cartilaginous chamber enclosing the olfactory sac is laterally adjacent to the anterior rostral tube (art; fig. 2, 4) and anterior to the posterior inferior rostral tube (pit; fig. 2, 5). The olfactory sac is complexly folded. Its lateral wall is a simple mucous membrane lacking any olfactory receptors (lw; fig. 12A). Its medial wall, however, is deeply infolded into three dorsal lobes and two ventral lobes that are lined by a sensory epithelium (oe; fig. 4, 12A). Within each lobe the sensory epithelium is further infolded to form many sensory crypts (cr; fig. 12).

The axons of the olfactory receptor cells pass through the connective tissue between adjacent crypts, turn medially, and then collect into small fascicles. These fascicles form distinct bundles associated with each lobe. Five such bundles – one for each lobe of the organ – can be recognized in figure 12A (arrows) and figure 4 (I). The bundles of olfactory axons collect on the medial surface of the olfactory organ, then penetrate the dura mater to terminate in the immediately adjacent olfactory bulb (ob; fig. 12B). The olfactory nerves in *Latimeria* are thus extremely short. It appears that the bundles of olfactory fibers associated with the three dorsal lobes enter the olfactory bulb dorsally, whereas the two ventral bundles enter ventrally.

Careful examination of the olfactory epithelium and olfactory fascicles, bundles and nerves, as well as the olfactory bulb and associated meninges and connective tissue, revealed no sizable neurons that could be interpreted as the ganglion of the terminal nerve. If a terminal nerve exists in *Latimeria*, then its ganglionic cells must either be extremely small or they must be located further caudally within the brain. Neither the rostral body (rb; fig. 2A) nor any other more caudal portion of the forebrain was methodically searched, however no other nerves appear to enter the forebrain in this specimen.

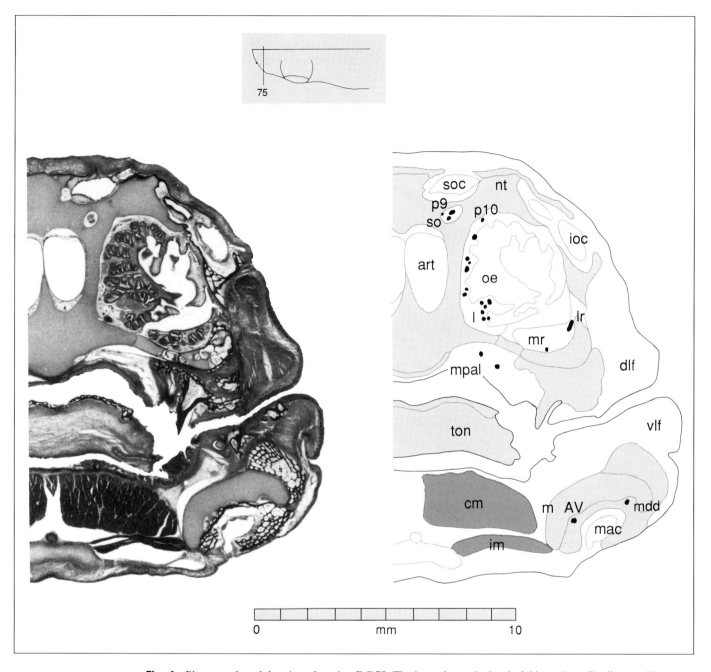

Fig. 4. Photograph and drawing of section RC 75. The inset shows the level of this section. Cartilage and bone are indicated by the light gray shading; darker shading indicates muscle. Nerves and their components are indicated by black. This section passes through the anterior rostral tube of the rostral organ (art), portions of the olfactory system (oe), and the supraorbital (soc), infraorbital (ioc) and mandibular (mac) cranial sensory canals. Additional structures and nerve components are discussed in the text and figure abbreviations.

Optic Nerve

The optic nerve arises from the retina at level RC 394. The optic head is located within the dorsal hemifield of the retina, approximately one-third of the distance from the dorsal margin of the eye. The nerve passes medially and obliquely through the sclera, towards the neurocranium, and is deeply folded or plicated along its length (fig. 2, 7). Throughout its course in the orbit, the optic nerve is ensheathed by an inner layer of loose connective tissue and

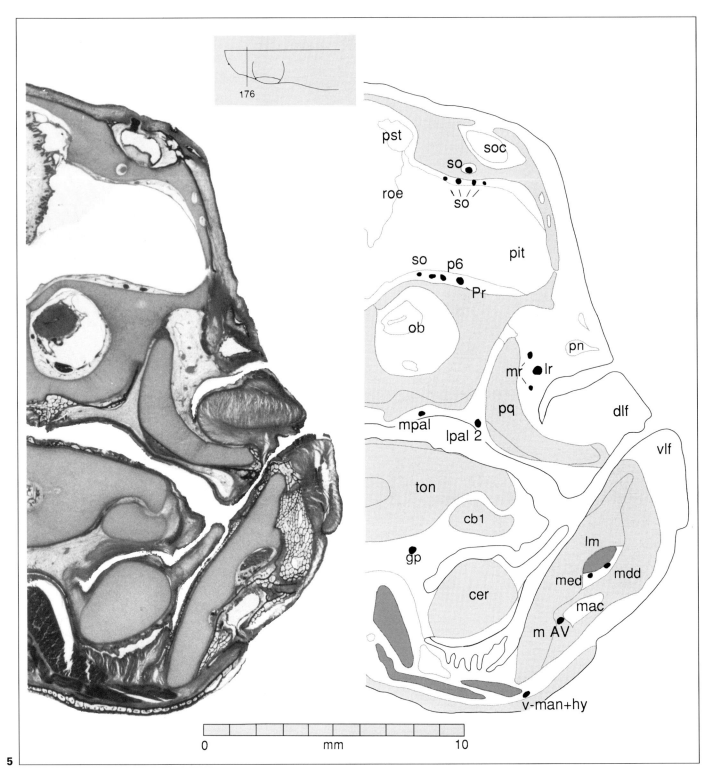

Fig. 5. Photograph and drawing of section RC 176. The inset shows the level of this section. The section passes through the posterior inferior rostral tube of the rostral organ (pit), the olfactory bulb (ob), the tongue (ton), ceratohyal (cer) and lower jaw.

Fig. 6. Photograph and drawing of section RC 296. The inset shows the level of this section. The section passes through the supraorbital (soc), infraorbital (ioc) and mandibular cranial sensory canals, the eye, three of the extrinsic ocular muscles (som, superior oblique muscle; iom, inferior oblique muscle; mrm, medial rectus muscle), and the first and second ceratobranchials (cb1 and cb2).

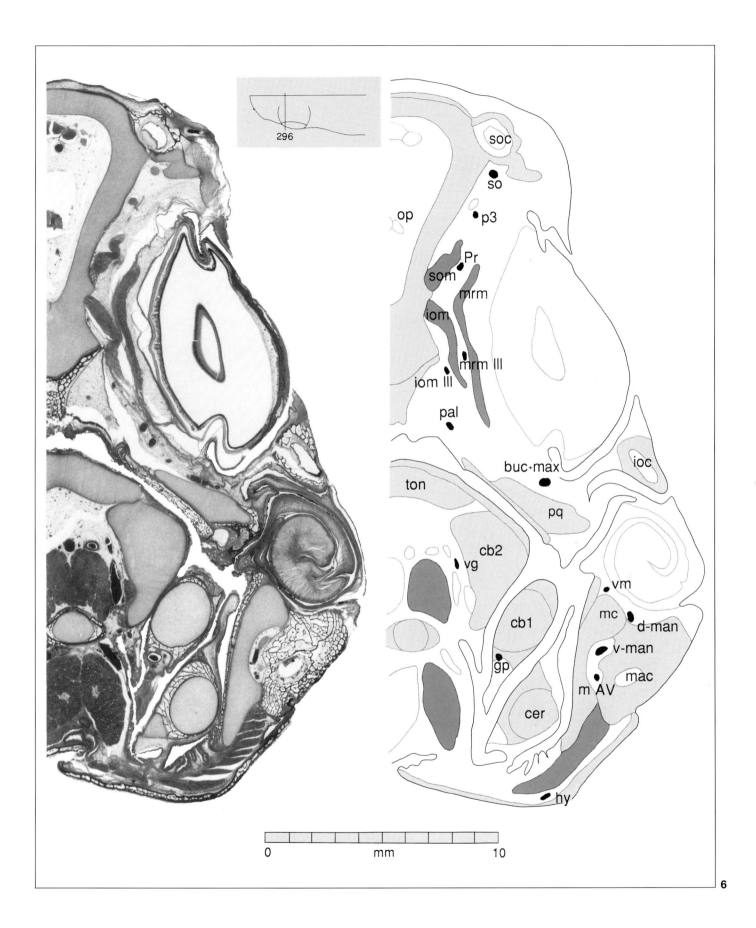

296

soc
so
op
p3
Pr
som
mrm
iom
mrm III
iom III
pal
buc+max
ioc
ton
pq
cb2
vg
vm
cb1
mc
d-man
v-man
gp
mac
m AV
cer
hy

0   mm   10

6

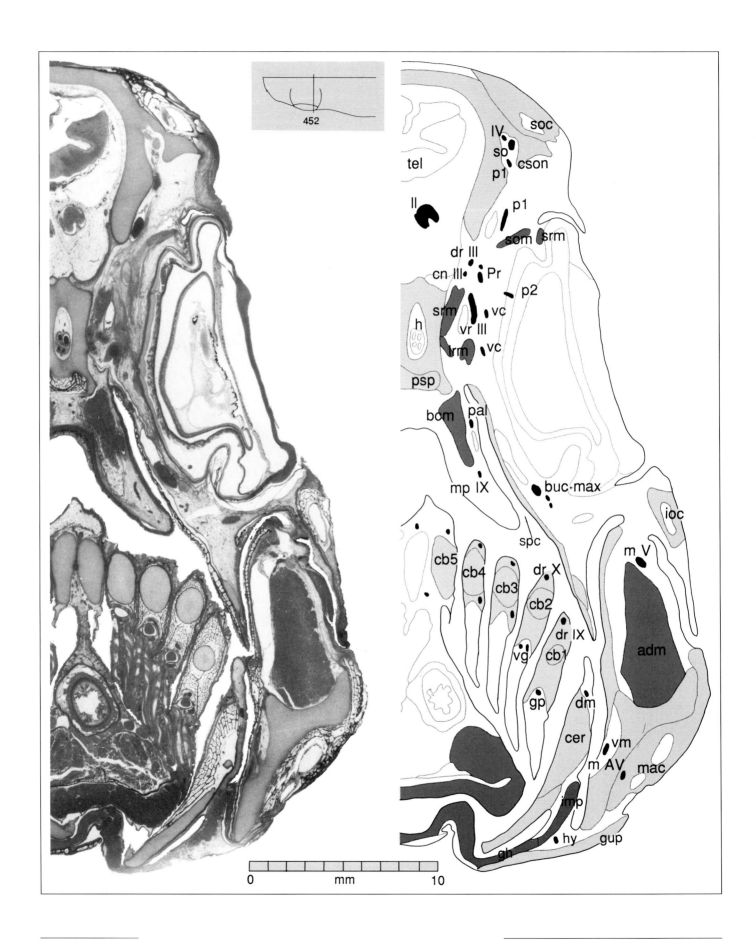

an outer fibrous layer. The outer fibrous layer is continuous with both the sclera and the perichondrium of the neurocranium, and it merges with the neurocranial perichondrium adjacent to the large optic foramen. The ophthalmic artery also exits the neurocranium via the optic foramen and travels with the optic nerve inside the fibrous sheath. Within the neurocranium, the optic nerve passes ventral to the telencephalic hemispheres (II; fig.2B, 7) where it decussates to form the floor of the preoptic area. The plication of the optic nerve is maintained as far caudally as the optic chiasm. The plication appears as an 'S' in transverse sections (fig.2). If one thinks of the 'S' as having a body, a dorsal arm, and a ventral arm, then it is the fibers in the body of the 'S' that decussate most rostrally. This occurs in the pup at about level RC 485. Missing sections near the junction of Blocks A and B in the pup prevented us from discerning the course of more caudally decussating optic fibers, however examination of the optic nerves and chiasm in sections of an adult specimen confirm that the rostral portion of the chiasm is formed by the body of the 'S'. In this same adult specimen, it is clear that the fibers of the ventral arms of the nerve are the next to decussate, approximately halfway through the rostrocaudal extent of the chiasm, and their interdigitation forms the ventral one-quarter of the chiasm. The fibers of the dorsal arms of the 'S' finally interdigitate to form the most caudal one-quarter of the chiasm. At this point the fibers of the bodies and the ventral arms already course dorsally and laterally to form the marginal optic tracts. All three portions contribute to the marginal optic tract, which subsequently courses dorsally and laterally over the surface of the telencephalon and midbrain.

Nerves of the Extraocular Muscles

The proximal courses of the motor nerves to the eye muscles are diagrammed in the main reconstruction (III, IV, VI; fig.2). The peripheral courses of these nerves and their muscles are diagrammed in figure 3. Because these nerves consist of motor fibers, they are indicated by red; the muscles are shaded differently according to their inner-

Fig. 7. Photograph and drawing of section RC 452. The inset shows the level of this section. The section passes through the telencephalon (tel), the opening of the posterior canal for the superficial ophthalmic ramus (cson), three of the extrinsic ocular muscles (som, superior oblique muscle; srm, superior rectus muscle; lrm, lateral rectus muscle), the hypophysis (h), basicranial muscle (bcm), adductor mandibulae muscle (adm) and portions of all five gill arches (cb1–cb5).

vation. For reference, this diagram also outlines the spiracular chamber (spc; fig.3) and ear (horizontal semicircular canal, hscc; posterior semicircular canal, pscc; saccule, sac; fig.3).

Oculomotor Nerve

The oculomotor nerve leaves the ventral surface of the midbrain between levels RC 625 and RC 632. At level RC 632, three fascicles, each containing several smaller bundles, are seen. As more and more fibers leave the midbrain to join the nerve, distinctions among individual fascicles blur and disappear entirely more rostrally.

The oculomotor nerve has a winding course through the cranial cavity. Initially it is located just dorsal to the intracranial venous sinus and medial to the profundal ganglion (III, g Pr; fig.8). At this point the connective tissue ensheathing the oculomotor nerve is much thinner than the sheath encapsulating the profundal ganglion. Ciliary ganglion cells are located in the body of the oculomotor nerve, beginning at level RC 598 and continuing rostrally to level RC 576 (cg; fig.2A, 3). These cells are especially easy to see in section RC 583, where they form the lateral border of the nerve (fig.13B,C). Except for these ganglion cells, the nerve appears as a single, undivided bundle. Rostral to the ciliary ganglion, the oculomotor nerve passes lateral to the hypothalamus (levels RC 549 to RC 523), and by level RC 515 its sheath begins to thicken as it approaches its foramen in the wall of the braincase. Still inside the cranium the oculomotor nerve begins to subdivide into dorsal and ventral rami by about level RC 510 (vr III, dr III; fig.3). These two rami pass together through a distinct foramen in the basisphenoid [Millot and Anthony, 1958, plate 27] and emerge in the back of the orbit at level RC 491. In the pup, the passage of the oculomotor nerve through the braincase occurs just at the break between Blocks A and B.

Within the orbit, the dorsal ramus immediately subdivides into dorsal and ventral ramules which follow very tortuous paths. The dorsal ramule (srm III; fig.3) subdivides at level RC 471 into dorsal and ventral elements which further subdivide into fine divisions, all of which remain within a common sheath of connective tissue. Eventually, all components of the dorsal ramule of the dorsal ramus of the oculomotor nerve enter the posterodorsal border of the superior rectus muscle (levels RC 439-RC 431, srm III, srm; fig.3).

The ventral ramule of the dorsal ramus contributes fibers to the ciliary 'nerves' by a complicated route. Initially, the ramule continues rostrally in the orbit, but at

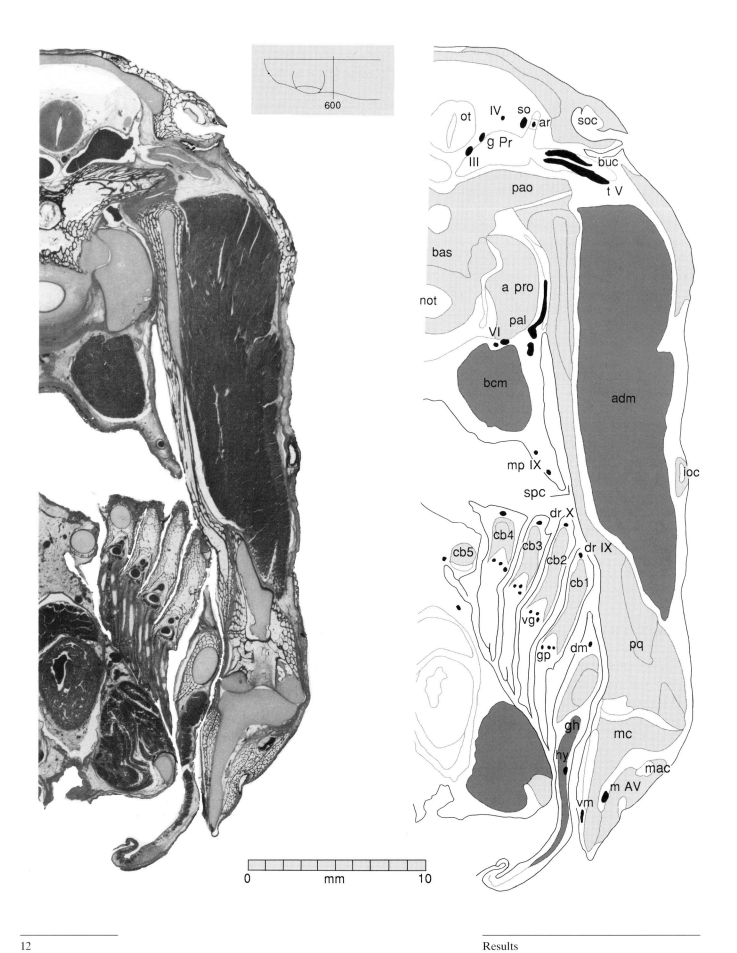

600

IV
so
ot
ar
soc
g Pr
III
buc
t V
pao
bas
a pro
not
pal
VI
bcm
adm
mp IX
ioc
spc
dr X
cb4
cb3
cb5
cb2
dr IX
cb1
vg
dm
pq
gp
gh
mc
ny
mac
m AV
vm

0   mm   10

level RC 452, it veers laterally into the plane of connective tissue of the superior rectus muscle (cn III; fig. 3). It then perforates the muscle at level RC 447 to join a profundal ramule (p2; fig. 2A), which lies just lateral to the superior rectus muscle. Shortly thereafter, this ramule gives rise to the dorsal and ventral ciliary 'nerves' (p2, vc; fig. 7, 13).

The ventral ramus of the oculomotor nerve (vr III; fig. 3) continues rostrally in the orbit, turning sharply ventromedially at about level RC 460, near the divergence of the orbitonasal vein and the orbital venous sinus system. By level RC 431, the ventral ramus passes the lateral edge of the inferior rectus muscle (irm; fig. 3), and it innervates this muscle at level RC 427 (irm III; fig. 3) via a dorsomedially directed ramule. This ramule continues rostrally on the dorsolateral surface of the inferior rectus muscle as far as level RC 409 (irm III; fig. 3).

The remaining fibers of the ventral ramus of the oculomotor nerve continue rostrally and medially along the ventral surface of the inferior rectus muscle (levels RC 425 to RC 375; fig. 3). The ramus then turns laterally, and, by level RC 351, it approaches the ventral border of the medial rectus muscle (mrm; fig. 3). It parallels the border of the medial rectus muscle as it continues rostrally and laterally until about level RC 325. Here it splits into medial and lateral ramules (iom III, mrm III; fig. 3). The medial ramule passes along the ventromedial border of the inferior oblique muscle, which it innervates (iom III, iom; fig. 3). The lateral ramule ramifies in the ventromedial border of the medial rectus muscle, ending at about level RC 275 (mrm III, mrm; fig. 3).

Trochlear Nerve

The root of the trochlear nerve arises dorsally at the junction of the midbrain and cerebellum at level RC 679 (IV; fig. 2). The nerve continues forward through the dorsal portion of the cranial cavity to about level RC 460 where it passes through its own foramen in the pleurosphenoid portion of the sphenethmoid cartilage to enter the posterior canal for the superficial ophthalmic ramus of the anterodorsal lateral line nerve (IV; fig. 7). At level RC 452, the trochlear nerve enters the orbit, as the canal for the superficial ophthalmic ramus opens. The nerve descends slightly, passes dorsal to the superior rectus muscle, and contacts

the superior oblique muscle at level RC 388 (som; fig. 3). The nerve then continues rostrally on the dorsal surface of the superior oblique muscle and ramifies between levels RC 325 and RC 310 (fig. 3).

Abducent Nerve

As reported earlier [Bemis and Northcutt, 1991], the abducent nerve of *Latimeria* innervates the basicranial muscle as well as the lateral rectus muscle. This unique pattern involves the relatively posterior exit of the abducent nerve from the neurocranium, its long course along the dorsal surface of the basicranial muscle, and its subsequent ascent into the orbit to ramify in the lateral rectus muscle (VI, lrm; fig. 3). We include much of our previous description for completeness.

The abducent nerve originates from the ventral surface of the medulla, between levels RC 855 and RC 860 (VI; fig. 2) and can be traced rostrally into a foramen defined by the medial wall of the otic capsule and notochordal connective tissues. At level RC 851, the nerve is enclosed by cartilage on three sides, with the medial wall of its foramen still composed of connective tissue. A small blood vessel travels together with the nerve.

At level RC 820 (VI; fig. 3, 10), the abducent nerve lies within the otic capsule, medial to the saccule. It passes rostrally, pressed ventrally against the medial wall of the otic capsule. By level RC 800, the nerve is in a small depression in the cartilage of the wall, which ventrally becomes a well defined foramen in the cartilaginous ventral wall of the otic capsule by level RC 771. Further ventrally (VI; fig. 9), the nerve passes through the trabecular ossifications of the prootic bone (level RC 680) and appears on the dorsal surface of the basicranial muscle by level RC 671 (indicated by p on fig. 3; the relationships of VI at this point are exemplified by section RC 600 in fig. 8).

The abducent nerve innervates the basicranial muscle along most of its length. This is achieved in part by a large, caudally directed ramus (r VI; fig. 3) which is obvious at level RC 730 (r VI; fig. 9) and which extends caudally at least as far as level RC 810. There are also several other rami that leave the main trunk of the nerve. These include a large medial ramus (m VI; fig. 3) which, in turn, gives rise to two large recurrent ramules which enter the main mass of the basicranial muscle and divide repeatedly before disappearing as discrete bundles. A small lateral recurrent ramus leaves the main trunk of the nerve at level RC 630 and continues along the dorsolateral border of the muscle as far caudally as level RC 663.

Fig. 8. Photograph and drawing of section RC 600. The inset shows the level of this section. The section passes through the adductor mandibulae (adm) and basicranial (bcm) muscles as well as the jaw joint (between the palatoquadrate, pq, and Meckel's cartilage, mc).

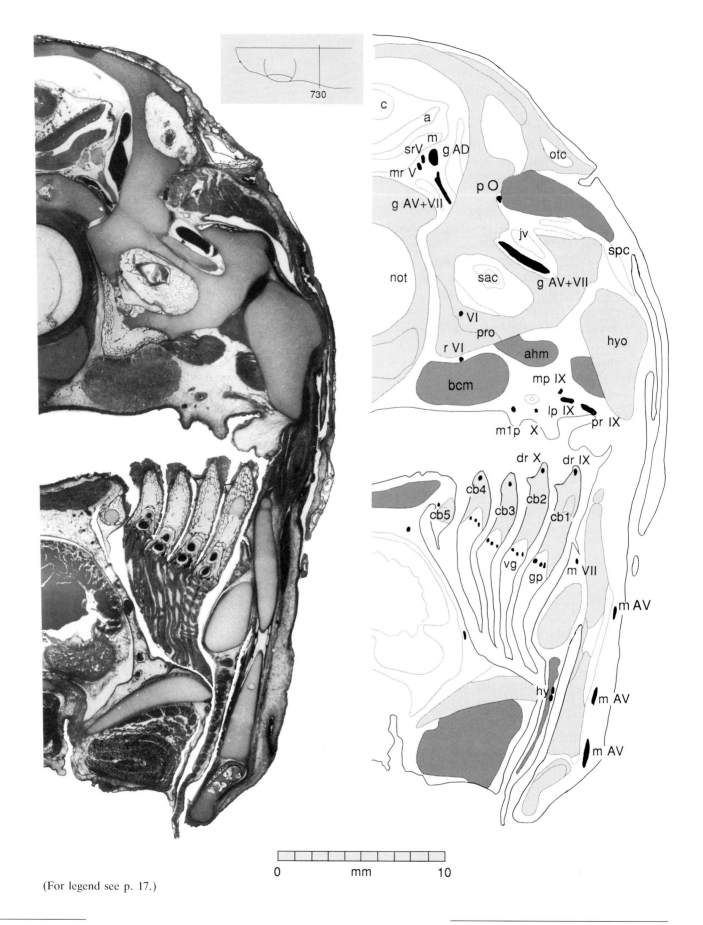

730

(For legend see p. 17.)

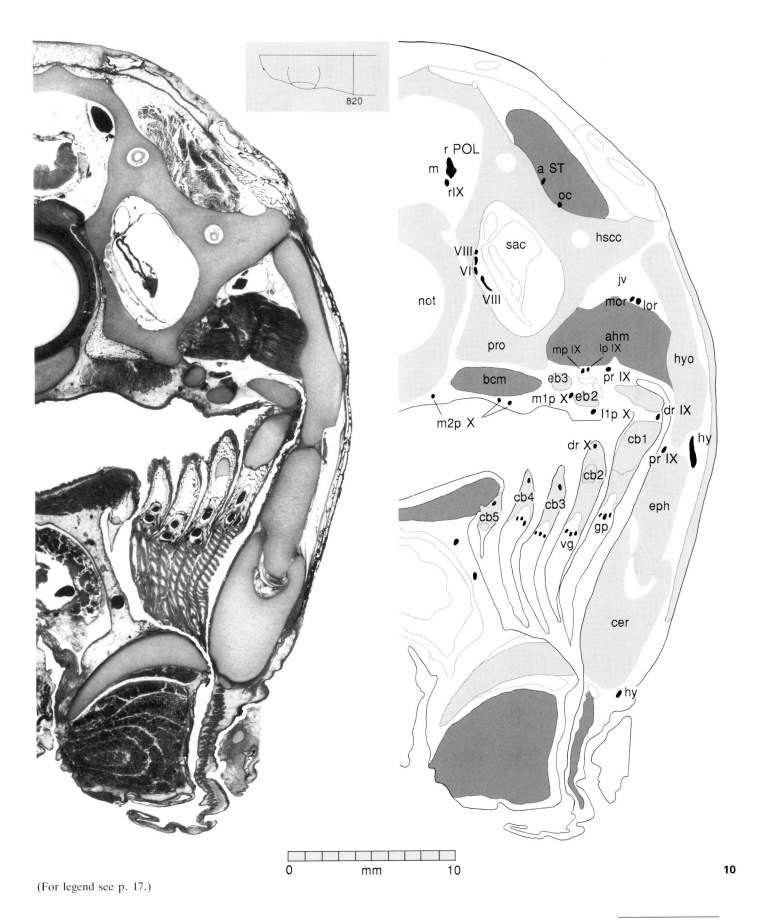

820

r POL
m
a ST
rIX
oc
hscc
VIII
sac
VI
jv
VIII
mor
lor
not
pro
ahm
hyo
mp IX
lp IX
bcm
eb3
pr IX
m1p X
eb2
l1p X
dr IX
m2p X
cb1
hy
dr X
pr IX
cb2
eph
cb4
cb3
cb5
gp
vg
cer
hy

0   mm   10

(For legend see p. 17.)

10

15

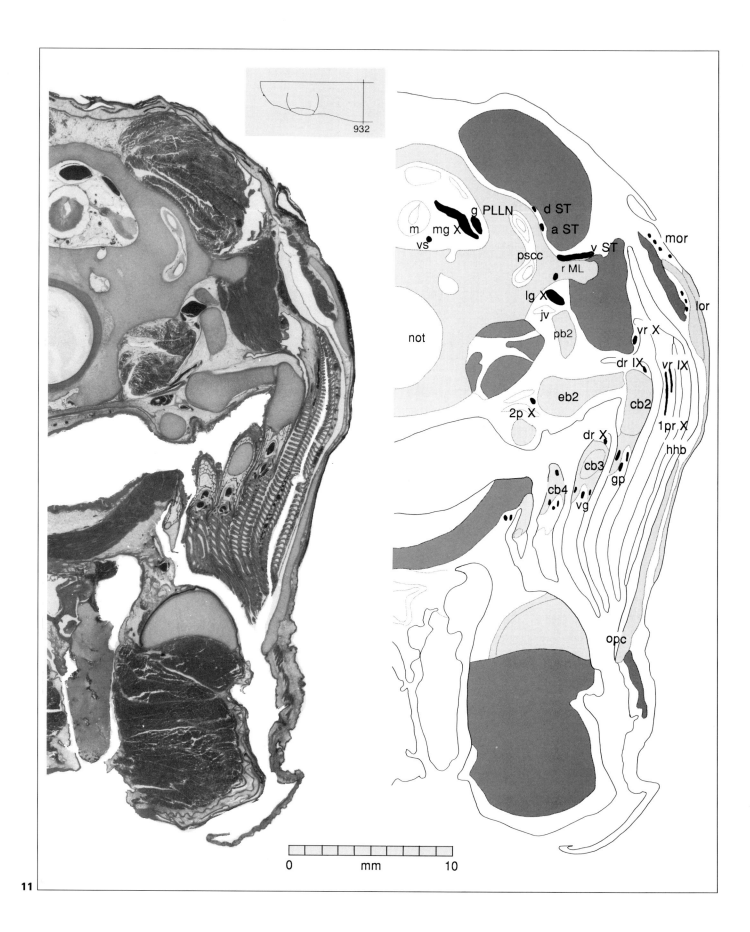

932

0   mm   10

Between levels RC 635 and RC 620, the medial ramus (m VI; fig. 3) passes anteromedially on the dorsal surface of the basicranial muscle and issues several smaller ramules. This is the midpoint of the muscle and the major site of innervation. The medial ramus continues to arborize rostrally.

The balance of the abducent nerve continues forward on the dorsal surface of the basicranial muscle as a well defined bundle (VI, bcm; fig. 8). Only a few small motor branches enter the basicranial muscle here. In this region, the abducent nerve lies medial to the palatine ramus of the facial nerve (pal; fig. 8). The abducent nerve leaves the muscle (ac; fig. 3) and begins to pass dorsally and laterally along the anterolateral surface of the prootic cartilage. By section RC 488, the abducent nerve has completed its lateral passage of the prootic, and the nerve soon enters the back of the orbit.

At level RC 486, the abducent nerve passes between two major sinuses of the orbital venous sinus system, dorsal to the lateral rectus muscle (lrm; fig. 3). Final division of the nerve begins as it approaches the posterodorsal edge of the lateral rectus muscle (level RC 475), and three ramules can be traced anteriorly from level RC 472 to level RC 460. The medial ramule courses along the dorsal surface of the muscle. The lateral ramule enters the belly of the muscle at level RC 470. The central ramule directly enters and ramifies in the lateral rectus muscle (fig. 3).

Profundal Nerve

Throughout its entire extent, the ganglion, root and rami of the profundal nerve are entirely separate from the trigeminal nerve. The sensory neurons of the profundal ganglion are similar to those of the trigeminal ganglion in that both are smaller and more darkly stained than the ganglionic cells of the anterodorsal lateral line nerve or the anteroventral lateral line nerve (g Pr, g AD; fig. 13B, 14A, B, D, 15B). The ganglion of the profundal nerve is extremely long, and most of it is intracranial. The ganglion begins at level RC 675 and ends at level RC 500. The proximal portion of the profundal ganglion is closely associated with the trigeminal ganglion and lies along its medial edge (g Pr, g V; fig. 2A, 14A, 14C). As the profundal ganglion is traced rostrally, it moves medially and ventrally to lie adjacent to the lateral edge of the oculomotor nerve (g Pr, III; fig. 2A, 8). Throughout their rostral continuation in the neurocranium, the profundal ganglion and oculomotor nerve retain this topographic relationship. At level RC 551, the profundal ganglion veers ventrally and laterally to enter its foramen through the spongy prootic bone. The ganglion passes laterally, exiting the neurocranium and emerging in the orbit at the level of RC 520. The most rostral cells of the profundal ganglion are located at the level of RC 490. The peripheral cell processes of the profundal ganglion continue rostrally as the profundal ramus (Pr; fig. 2A), which gives rise to ten ramules as it courses toward the tip of the snout. The centrally coursing cell processes of the sensory neurons of the profundal ganglion form a single sensory root which runs medially adjacent to the sensory ganglion and roots of the trigeminal nerve (fig. 2A). The root passes ventral to the auricular leaves of the cerebellum and enters the medulla immediately rostral to the sensory and motor roots of the trigeminal nerve (RC levels 725 to 750; fig. 2).

As the profundal ramus is traced rostrally, its first ramule (p1; fig. 2A, 7) arises from the dorsal surface of the ramus at level RC 475. This ramule courses dorsally, lateral to the orbital venous sinus (p1; fig. 7), and passes through a foramen in the floor of the posterior canal for the superficial ophthalmic ramus in the sphenethmoid cartilage. Ramule p1 corresponds to the branch termed 'posterior interophthalmic anastomosis' by Millot and Anthony [1965; their fig. 21]. Study of the sections, however, confirms that ramule p1 passes medial to the superficial ophthalmic ramus without exchanging fibers and promptly exits the canal through a foramen in the roof of the canal for the superficial ophthalmic ramus to innervate the overlying skin.

Immediately rostral to the origin of p1, a second ramule arises from the ventral surface of the profundal ramus (p2, RC 450; fig. 2A). This second ramule, approximately half of the diameter of the profundal ramus, turns ventrally and laterally and divides into dorsal and ventral ciliary nerves

Fig. 9. Photograph and drawing of section RC 730. The inset shows the level of this section. The section passes through the hyomandibula (hyo) and its adductor muscle (ahm) as well as the rostralmost portion of the saccule. The course of the recurrent ramus of the abducent nerve (r VI) is indicated dorsal to the basicranial muscle. Several segments of the mandibular ramus of the anteroventral lateral line nerve (m AV) are apparent because this nerve passes nearly vertically in its descent to the lower jaw.

Fig. 10. Photograph and drawing of section RC 820. The inset shows the level of this section. The section passes through three skeletal elements of the hyoid arch: the hyomandibula (hyo), epihyal (eph), and ceratohyal (cer). The saccule (sac) and portions of the semicircular canals (e.g., hscc) are also indicated.

Fig. 11. Photograph and drawing of section RC 932. The inset shows the level of this section. The section passes through the caudal portions of the posterior semicircular canal (pscc), skeletal elements of the second gill arch (pharyngobranchial 2, epibranchial 2, and ceratobranchial 2), and the hyoidean hemibranch (hhb).

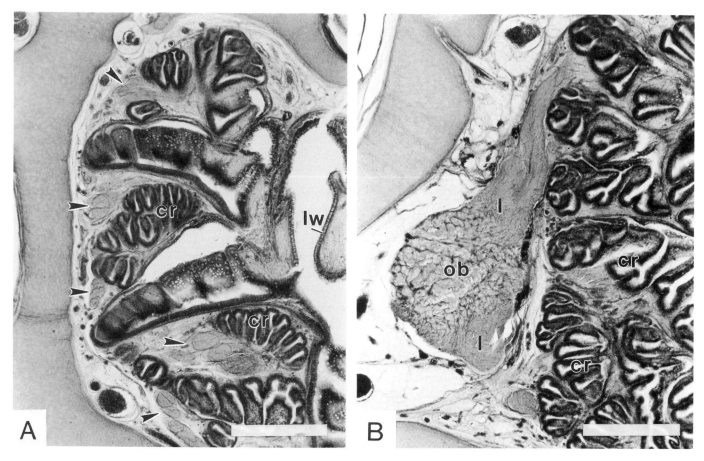

Fig. 12. Plate of left olfactory nerve and epithelium. Dorsal and medial above and to left, respectively. **A** Olfactory sac showing five bundles of the olfactory nerve (arrowheads) in section RC 70. The smooth lateral wall (lw) and olfactory crypts (cr) of the sac are indicated. **B** Olfactory nerve (I) and implantation cone into the olfactory bulb (ob), section RC 130. Scale bar equals 1 mm.

which penetrate the sclera dorsomedially (RC 452; fig. 7, 13A) and ventromedially (level RC 467), respectively. Where p2 divides into the dorsal and ventral ciliary nerves, it is joined by a branch of the oculomotor nerve that probably consists of the axons of the ciliary ganglion. The ciliary ganglion is embedded in the proximal portion of the oculomotor nerve (cg; fig. 2B, 3, 13B). Further details and discussion of the anastomosis between oculomotor and profundal rami are described under the section on the oculomotor nerve and in the Discussion.

As the profundal ramus descends through the orbit, it lies directly dorsal to the lateral rectus muscle, near the terminal arborization of the abducent nerve. This is especially obvious at level RC 475. It then hooks sharply around the anterior edge of the lateral rectus muscle and occupies a position deep in the orbit. Further rostrally, it moves medially and passes dorsal to the optic nerve (Pr, level RC 400; fig. 2A). The profundal ramus lies about halfway between

the sclera of the eye and the sphenethmoid cartilage, surrounded by the loose connective tissue of the orbit. At level RC 350, the profundal ramus gives rise to another dorsally coursing ramule (p3; fig. 2A, 6). Ramule p3 passes through the superior oblique muscle to enter the anterior canal for the superficial ophthalmic ramus in the sphenethmoid cartilage. Ramule p3 passes medial to and does not anastomose with the superficial ophthalmic ramus. It penetrates the roof of the anterior canal for the superficial ophthalmic ramus through a small foramen and innervates the overlying skin.

After giving rise to p3, the profundal ramus moves laterally (Pr; fig. 2A) and enters a groove in the medial wall of the orbit (level RC 250). As it enters this groove, a laterally directed ramule arises (p4; fig. 2A). Slightly rostral, the groove in the sphenethmoid cartilage becomes enclosed as the canal for the profundal ramus; this canal provides a passage for the ramus through the postnasal wall and into the

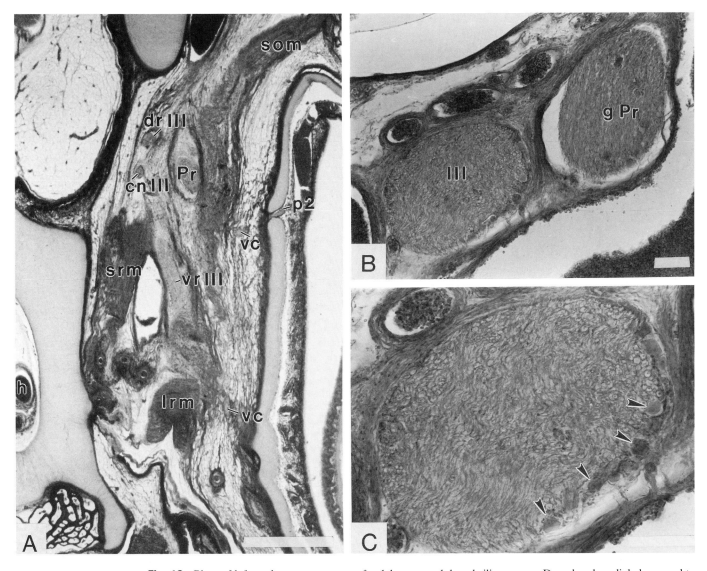

Fig. 13. Plate of left oculomotor nerve, profundal nerve and dorsal ciliary nerve. Dorsal and medial above and to left, respectively. **A** Contents of orbit in section RC 452 (also see fig. 7). The superior oblique (som), superior rectus (srm) and lateral rectus muscles (lrm) are indicated as well as the dorsal ciliary nerve (p2) and two sections through the ventral ciliary nerve (vc). Scale bar equals 10 mm. **B** Section through oculomotor nerve (III) at level of ciliary ganglion, section RC 583. The ganglion of the profundal nerve (g Pr) is also indicated. Scale bar equals 1 mm. **C** Detail of ciliary ganglion cells in the same section, RC 583. Scale bar equals 1 mm.

region of the rostral organ. The laterally coursing ramule p4 divides into dorsal and ventral elements at the level of RC 224. At level RC 200, the dorsal element has divided into three mediolaterally arrayed divisions. The most lateral of these three divisions terminates in the caudal portion of the membranous wall of the posterior superior rostral tube at level RC 205 (pst; fig. 2A). The intermediate division terminates in the anterior membranous wall of the posterior superior rostral tube. The most medial division terminates in the overlying skin.

The ventral element of ramule p4 courses along the postnasal cartilage medial to the sclera of the eye; it penetrates the postnasal wall at the level of RC 220 to innervate the caudal membranous wall of the posterior inferior rostral tube. We saw no evidence that any of the divisions of ramule p4 innervates the rostral sac.

The profundal ramus continues rostrally through its foramen in the postnasal wall, and at the level of RC 200 it passes ventral to the posterior superior rostral tube (pst; fig. 2A). At level RC 198, a dorsolaterally directed ramule

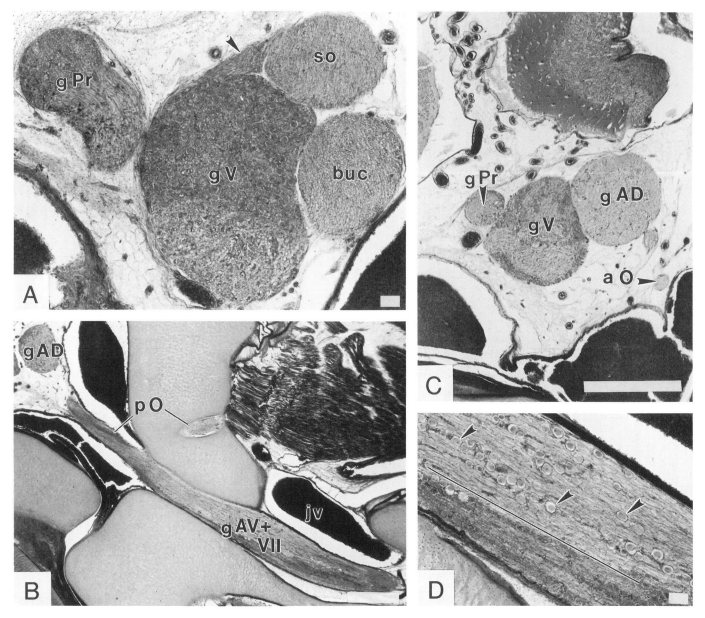

Fig. 14. Anterodorsal and anteroventral lateral line nerves and closely associated nerves. Dorsal and medial above and to left, respectively. **A** The ganglia of the profundal (g Pr) and trigeminal (g V) nerves lie medially adjacent to the superficial ophthalmic (so) and buccal (buc) rami of the anterodorsal lateral line nerve. Sensory cell bodies are restricted to the dorsal half of the trigeminal ganglion, with trigeminal motor fibers occurring in the ventral half. The arrowhead indicates somatosensory trigeminal fibers that anastomose with the first ramule of the superficial ophthalmic ramus. Medial is to left of field. Level RC 660. Scale bar equals 1 mm. **B** Ganglia of anteroventral lateral line nerve + facial nerve (g AV + VII) lying within the jugular canal. The posterior ramus of the otic nerve (pO) is also shown exiting the neurocranium, as well as the caudal pole of the ganglion of the anterodorsal lateral line nerve (g AD). Level RC 727, scale bar equals 1 mm. **C** Section through ganglia of the anterodorsal lateral line nerve (g AD), trigeminal nerve (g V), and profundal nerve (g Pr) demonstrating that they are separate structures. Level RC 690, scale bar equals 1 mm. **D** Higher magnification of the fused ganglia of the anteroventral lateral line and facial nerves showing distinct differences in the size and staining of the sensory neurons. The large, palely stained cell bodies indicated with arrowheads occur in lateral line ganglia; the smaller cell bodies occur in all visceral sensory ganglia. Level RC 727, scale bar equals 1 mm.

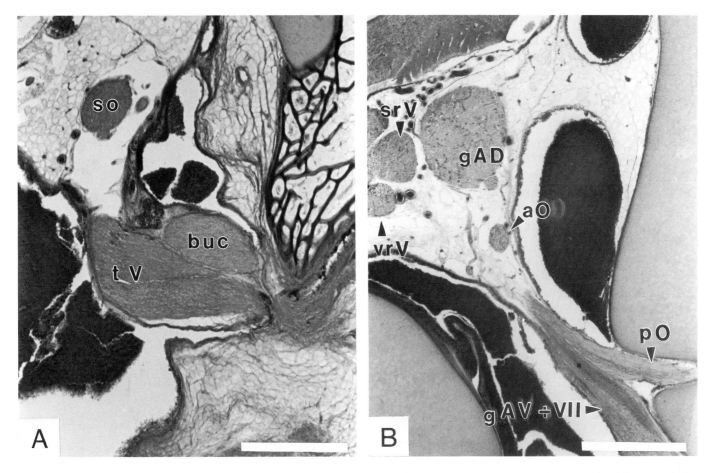

Fig. 15. Proximal relations of the anterodorsal lateral line nerve. Dorsal and medial above and to left, respectively. **A** Buccal ramus of anterodorsal lateral line nerve (buc) and trigeminal trunk (t V) near exit from neurocranium. The trigeminal trunk is nearing its subdivision into maxillary and mandibular rami; the maxillary ramus subsequently anastomoses with the buccal ramus of the anterodorsal lateral line nerve to form the buccal + maxillary complex. The superficial ophthalmic ramus of the anterodorsal lateral line nerve (so) also is indicated. Level RC 617, scale equals 1 mm. **B** The posterior ramus of the otic lateral line nerve (p O) is entirely separate from the fused ganglia of the anteroventral + facial nerves (g AV + VII). The ganglion of the anterodorsal lateral line nerve (g AD) and the sensory (sr V) and motor roots (vr V) of the trigeminal nerve are also indicated. Level RC 720, scale bar equals 1 mm.

(p5; fig.2A) arises and passes along the caudal membranous wall of the posterior inferior rostral tube (pit; fig.2A). Ramule p5 then passes dorsally through a foramen in the cartilage to innervate the overlying skin. It may also innervate the caudal membranous wall of the posterior inferior rostral tube, but this is not certain. We believe that ramule p5 probably corresponds to the dorsal lateral ramule of the profundal ramus diagrammed by Millot and Anthony [1965; their fig.21].

As the profundal ramus continues rostrally, it lies immediately ventral to the membranous wall of the posterior inferior rostral tube. At level RC 181, it gives off a medially directed ramule (p6; fig.2A) which innervates the ventral membranous wall of the posterior inferior rostral tube (pit,

p6; fig.5). At level RC 164, another laterally directed ramule (p7; fig.2A) innervates the anterior membranous wall of the posterior inferior rostral tube.

At level RC 155, the profundal ramus re-enters a canal in the ethmoid cartilage and continues rostrally to enter the olfactory capsule at level RC 139. It then gives rise to a dorsally directed ramule (p8; fig.2A) which passes through the cartilage to innervate the membranous wall of the anterior rostral tube (art; fig.2A) and then proceeds dorsally to innervate the overlying skin. Ramule p8 probably corresponds to the dorsal interior ramule of Millot and Anthony [1965; their fig. 21].

The profundal ramus continues rostrally along the dorsomedial edge of the olfactory sac where it divides into a medial ramule (p9; fig.2A, 4) and a lateral ramule (p10; fig.2A, 4). Ramule p9 enters the ethmoid cartilage and courses dorsally to enter the anterior canal for the superficial ophthalmic ramus at level RC 76 where its fibers remain separated from those of the superficial ophthalmic ramus by a small blood vessel. The fibers of ramule p9 then course medially, exit the canal via a small foramen, and terminate in the skin medial and posterior to the posterior ethmoid commissure.

Ramule p10 divides into medial and lateral elements at level RC 72. The lateral element subsequently terminates in the overlying skin at level RC 48. The medial element divides into dorsal and ventral divisions at level RC 62. The dorsal division of the medial element terminates in the skin of the snout. The ventral division divides into three branches which also innervate the skin of the snout.

In summary, the profundal nerve appears to be solely a somatosensory nerve that innervates the skin of the snout and the membranes of the rostral tubes. There is no evidence for profundal innervation of the rostral sac of the rostral organ, nor are there any anastomoses with branches of

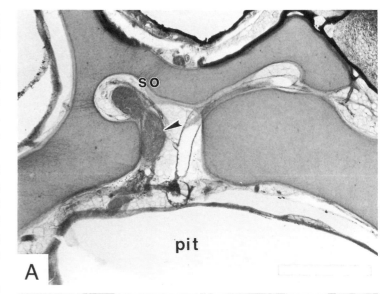

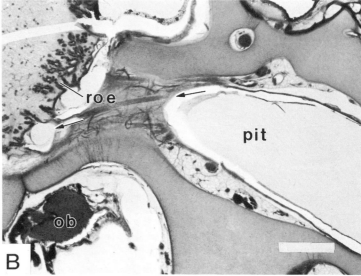

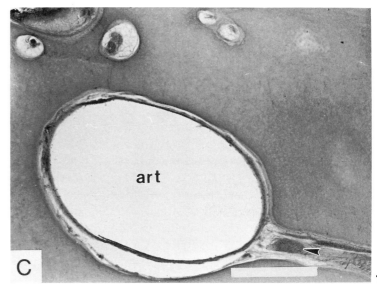

Fig. 16. Innervation of the rostral organ. Dorsal and medial above and to left, respectively. **A** The superficial ophthalmic ramus of the anterodorsal lateral line nerve (so) passes dorsally to the posterior inferior rostral tube (pit). The arrowhead indicates one of two ramules of the superficial ophthalmic ramus running over the dorsal surface of the epithelium of the posterior inferior rostral tube. Level RC 188, scale bar equals 1 mm. **B** Elements of the ramule shown in A, ramifying as they pass medially to reach the rostral sac associated with the posterior inferior rostral tube. Level RC 184, scale bar equals 1 mm. **C** Lateral ramule of the buccal + maxillary complex (arrowhead) as it passes medially beneath the floor of the anterior rostral tube (art) to innervate the epithelium of the rostral sac associated with that tube. Level RC 36, scale bar equals 1 mm.

Fig. 17. Ganglia and relationships of the middle lateral line nerve, the supratemporal lateral line nerve, and the posterior lateral line nerve. Dorsal and medial above and to left, respectively. **A** Relationship of ganglion of the middle lateral line nerve (g MLLN) to the trunk (t IX) and lateral ganglion of the glossopharyngeal nerve (lg IX). The ganglion of the middle lateral line nerve is distinct from those of the glossopharyngeal nerve. Level RC 901, scale bar equals 1 mm. **B** The ganglion of the posterior lateral line nerve (g PLLN) occurs as a distinct ganglion lateral to the medial ganglion (mg X) and trunk (t X) of the vagal nerve. Level RC 929, scale bar equals 1 mm. **C** The ganglion of the supratemporal lateral line nerve (g ST) is separate from the ganglion of the posterior lateral line nerve (g PLLN) except along its ventromedial border (indicated by fine straight lines). Both ganglia lie dorsolateral to the vagal trunk (T X). Level RC 938, scale bar equals 1 mm. **D** Relationships of the supratemporal lateral line nerve (ST), the posterior lateral line nerve (PLLN), and the vagal trunk (t X) as they exit the neurocranium. The lateral ganglion of the vagal nerve (lg X) clearly lies outside the neurocranium. Level RC 954, scale bar equals 1 mm.

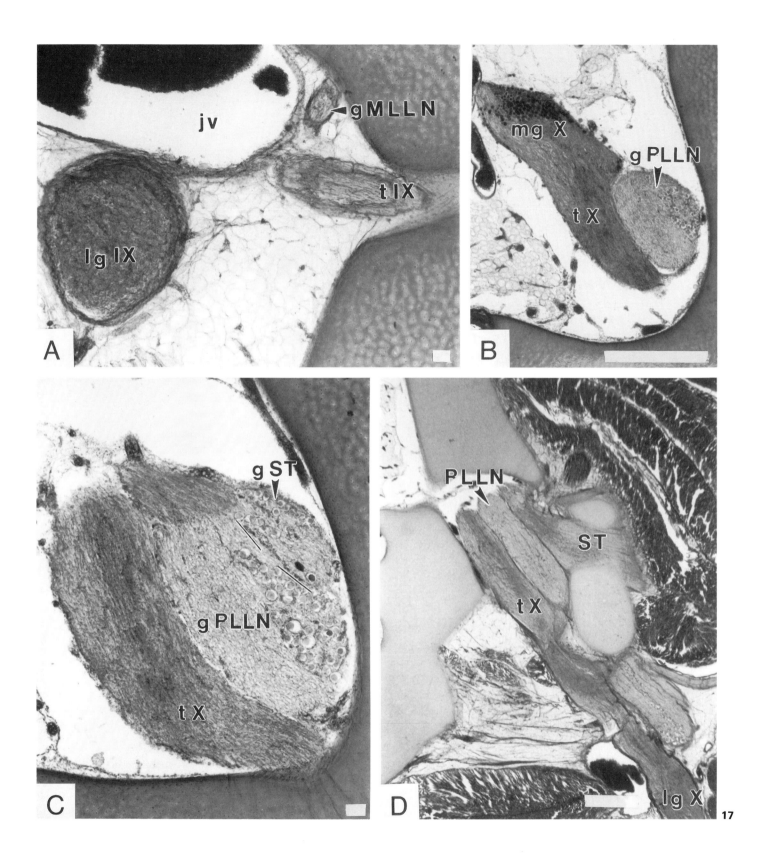

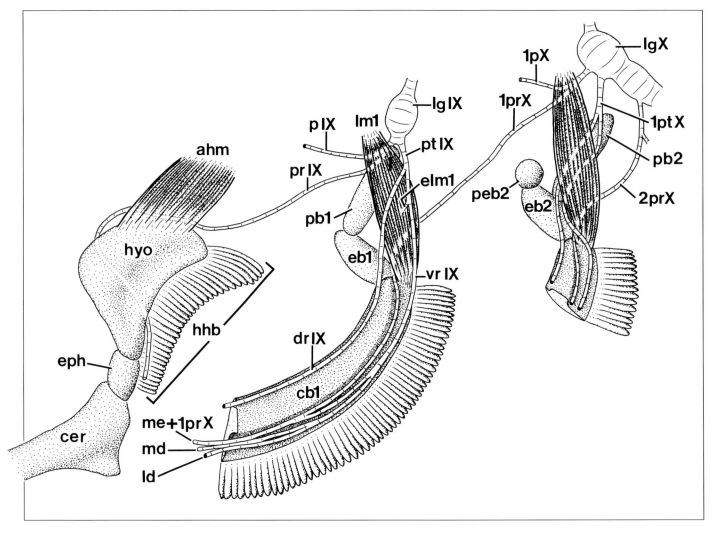

Fig. 18. Schematic lateral interpretation of skeleton, muscles and nerves of the hyoid, glossopharyngeal and first vagal gill arches of the left side of the head. The distance between adjacent arches has been exaggerated. The diagram emphasizes the relationships and branching pattern of pretrematic and posttrematic rami of the glossopharyngeal nerve.

the anterodorsal lateral line nerve or the trigeminal nerve. The dorsal and ventral ciliary nerves appear to comprise fibers of the profundal nerve as well as fibers from the ciliary ganglion.

Trigeminal Nerve

The sensory ganglion of the trigeminal nerve in *Latimeria* is located entirely within the cranium. It has distinct sensory and motor roots and separate maxillary and mandibular rami. Unlike the condition reported in many other anamniotes, the superficial ophthalmic ramus of the trigeminal nerve is poorly developed if it is present at all.

The rostral pole of the trigeminal ganglion begins at level RC 613 (level RC 617 is shown in fig. 15A), and its caudal pole occurs at level RC 705 (g V; fig. 2B). Rostrally the ganglionic cells and their processes are clearly restricted to the dorsal half of the ganglion, with the motor fibers occupying the ventral half (fig. 14A). As the ganglion is traced caudally, the ventrally located motor fibers are surrounded by sensory somata (g V; fig. 14C). More caudally still, the sensory somata are located in the middle of the ganglion, and the sensory and motor fibers are divided into three segments. At the caudal pole of the ganglion, the dorsal sensory root and ventral motor root are well-defined. Both roots enter the medulla between levels RC 725 to RC 741. The sensory root is compact, and its fibers

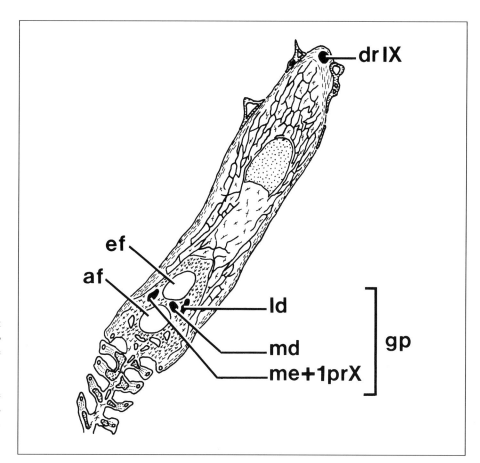

Fig. 19. Transverse section through first ceratobranchial bone and associated tissue to show typical innervation of gill arches. (See fig. 8, cb 1, for orientation of this diagram.) Nerves indicated derive from the posttrematic ramus of the glossopharyngeal nerve (dr IX, ld, md) and by fusion of elements with the first pretrematic ramus of the vagal nerve (me +1 prX). Efferent (ef) and afferent (af) branchial vessels are also indicated.

enter the medulla as a continuous sheet, whereas the motor root divides into five or six rootlets prior to entering the medulla. The trigeminal ganglion is bordered medially by the profundal ganglion and ramus, but these are distinctly separate as are their roots (g Pr, g V; fig. 2, 14C). Although the ganglionic cells of the profundal and trigeminal nerves are essentially the same size and have the same staining properties, the two ganglia and their roots have separate encapsulating sheaths and do not come into contact or exchange fibers. The trigeminal ganglion is bordered dorsolaterally by the ganglion and proximal portions of the rami of the anterodorsal lateral line nerve (g AD, g V; fig. 14C). The ganglion cells of the trigeminal nerve are generally smaller and stain more darkly than those of the anterodorsal ganglion, and they are entirely separate except for a short segment rostrally where peripheral processes of trigeminal neurons appear to pass through the anterodorsal ganglion to enter the anterior ramus of the otic lateral line nerve (levels RC 676 to RC 695; also see the sections on the anterodorsal lateral line nerve and the otic lateral line nerve).

The trigeminal fibers pass through the rostral pole of the anterodorsal ganglion, which almost immediately subdivides to form its superficial ophthalmic and buccal rami (level RC 660; arrowhead, so, buc; fig. 14A). At this point, sensory fibers of the trigeminal ganglion pass dorsal and ventral to the superficial ophthalmic ramus of the anterodorsal nerve, contributing to the first ramule of the superficial ophthalmic ramus and to the first ramule of the buccal ramus (also see description of superficial ophthalmic and buccal rami of anterodorsal lateral line nerve). These are the only trigeminal fibers innervating any part of the dorsomedial surface of the head and are homologous to the superficial ophthalmic ramus of the trigeminal nerve reported in other anamniotes (see Discussion).

The peripherally coursing fibers of the trigeminal sensory ganglion and the accompanying motor fibers form a lateroventrally directed trigeminal trunk from levels RC 613 to RC 595 (t V; fig. 2B, 8). As the trigeminal trunk passes rostrally within the neurocranium, it is closely associated with the buccal ramus of the anterodorsal lateral line nerve (fig. 2, 15A). As the trigeminal trunk exits the neurocranium (through the intracranial joint at level RC 620; see Millot and Anthony, 1965, fig. 20), the sensory fibers and motor fibers appear segregated in the dorsal and ventral halves of the trunk, respectively. By level RC 596, a sizable dorsomedial segment of the sensory component of the trigeminal trunk anastomoses with the overlying buccal ramus of the anterodorsal lateral line nerve. This segment constitutes the maxillary ramus of the trigeminal nerve (max; fig. 2B). From this point rostrally, the maxillary ramus of the trigeminal nerve and the buccal ramus of the anterodorsal lateral line nerve form a single bundle of fibers which we have termed the buccal + maxillary complex (buc + max; fig. 2A, 6, 7). The peripheral distribution of the buccal + maxillary complex is described in the section on the anterodorsal lateral line nerve (below).

The remaining fibers of the trigeminal trunk constitute the mandibular ramus of the trigeminal nerve (m V; fig. 2). The mandibular ramus continues ventrolaterally to pass over the dorsal border of the mandibular adductor muscle. The first ramule of the mandibular ramus arises from its medial border at level RC 598 (not shown in the reconstruction in fig. 2). This ramule turns medially, passes over the mandibular adductor muscle, and terminates in the palato-quadrate levator muscle at level RC 486. The second and third ramules arise from the medial surface of the ramus at level RC 598 as the ramus passes ventrally along the lateral edge of the mandibular adductor muscle. These ramules innervate the mandibular adductor muscle and also are not shown on the reconstruction. A fourth ramule arises from the medial edge of the ramus at level RC 519. As it passes over the ventrolateral edge of the mandibular adductor muscle, it innervates both the muscle and overlying skin. This is the only postorbital ramule of the mandibular ramus shown in our reconstruction (m4; fig. 2B).

As the mandibular ramus courses rostrally, it parallels the anterior edge of the mandibular adductor muscle. As the muscle extends ventrally to its insertion on the lower jaw, the nerve appears dorsal to the muscle fibers (m V; fig. 7). At level RC 313 the mandibular ramus divides into dorsal and ventral ramules (d-man and v-man; fig. 2B, 6). The dorsal ramule lies immediately lateral to Meckel's cartilage (d-man; fig. 6), whereas the ventral ramule lies in a shallow groove on the dorsolateral surface of Meckel's cartilage (v-man; fig. 6). By level RC 300, the ventral ramule of the mandibular ramus of the trigeminal nerve lies just dorsal to the ventral ramule of the mandibular ramus of the anteroventral lateral line nerve (v-man, m AV; fig. 2, 6).

Next we trace the rostral course of the dorsal ramule of the mandibular ramus (d-man; fig. 2B). The dorsal ramule travels rostrally, at the same level as the mandibular ramus

prior to its split (d-man; fig. 2B, 6), and subsequently divides into a small medial element and a larger lateral element at level RC 275 (med, led; fig. 2B). At level RC 263, the medial element of the dorsal ramule moves into a canal on the dorsal surface of Meckel's cartilage. By level RC 249, this canal passes ventrally across the lateral surface of Meckel's cartilage. The medial element and its canal can be traced rostrally and ventrally. At level RC 189, the medial element of the dorsal ramule divides into dorsal and ventral divisions (neither of these divisions of the medial element is shown in fig. 2B, nor are they labeled as separate divisions in fig. 5). The dorsal division passes dorsolaterally to innervate the small labial muscle (lm; fig. 5). The corresponding ventral division terminates in the dermal bone adjacent to the mandibular sensory canal.

Next, we return to the lateral element of the dorsal mandibular ramule of the trigeminal nerve (led; fig. 2B). At level RC 244, the lateral element of the dorsal ramule divides into medial and lateral divisions (mdd, ldd; fig. 2B). By level RC 236, the lateral division has subdivided into dorsal and ventral branches, which are not shown on the reconstruction. At level RC 200, these branches have moved dorsally to innervate the lower lip fold and adjacent tissue.

By level RC 175, the medial division of the lateral element of the dorsal mandibular ramule of the mandibular ramus of the trigeminal nerve passes forward in a groove on the surface of Meckel's cartilage (mdd; fig. 2B, 5). It continues rostrally and passes just lateral to the ventral edge of the labial muscle; it may innervate the labial muscle, although it is not diminished in size rostral to the muscle. After passing the rostral border of the labial muscle, the medial division splits into dorsal and ventral branches not diagrammed in the reconstruction which occupy separate grooves on the dorsolateral surface of Meckel's cartilage. The ventral branch terminates in the dermal bone adjacent to the mandibular lateral line canal near level RC 117. The dorsal branch continues rostrally, ramifying in the dermis as it passes to the tip of the lower jaw (mdd; fig. 2B, 4).

We now return to the ventral ramule of the mandibular ramus of the trigeminal nerve (v-man; fig. 2B) which lies in the groove of Meckel's cartilage dorsal to the mandibular ramus of the anteroventral lateral line nerve at level RC 296 (m AV, v-man; fig. 6). As the ventral ramule continues rostrally, it passes medial and ventral to the mandibular ramus of the anteroventral nerve and comes to lie dorsally adjacent to the posterior intermandibularis muscle. As it passes ventral to the muscle (e.g. at level RC 240), numerous elements arise and innervate the muscle. As the ramule continues rostrally, it occupies a position ventral to the posterior intermandibularis muscle on the lateral one-third of the muscle. The differentiation between nerve and surrounding connective tissue is poor at this point, and it is difficult to discern whether or not it ramifies in the dermis and gular plate. It is clear, however, that the ramule anastomoses with the hyoid ramus of the facial nerve at about level RC 250 (v-man+hy; fig.2B, 5). Fibers of the v-man+hy continue to level RC 175, innervating the anterior intermandibularis muscle and adjacent skin along the way.

Facial Nerve

In the section describing the octavolateralis nerves, we present data supporting our interpretation that one root, one population of the sensory ganglion cells, and one distal ramus of the classical facial nerve, constitute a phylogenetically and developmentally separate lateral line nerve which we term the anteroventral lateral line nerve. We consider that this anteroventral lateral line nerve is secondarily fused with portions of the facial nerve proper in *Latimeria* to form what we term the anteroventral + facial ganglion (g AV + VII; fig.2). Thus we consider that the facial nerve proper of *Latimeria* consists of a single dorsal sensory root, a single ventral motor root, a single morphological class of ganglionic cells, and four distal rami. There is a mediorostrally directed palatine ramus (pal; fig.2) plus three more laterally disposed rami, all of which arise from a single hyomandibular trunk (hym; fig.2A). Two of these lateral rami are rostrally and ventrally directed to supply the mandible and the hyoid arch (m VII, hy; fig.2B); a third is a caudally directed opercular ramus which innervates the skin and other structures of the opercular region.

The ganglionic cells of the combined anteroventral + facial ganglion consist of large, lightly staining cells and small, darkly staining cells (fig.14B, D). The larger cells are located dorsally, and this population extends the full medial to lateral extent of the ganglion, as indicated (g AV+VII) in figure 2A. These large cells are the only cell type in the ganglion to occur intracranially (fig.14B). The smaller cells are located ventrally and have a more restricted occurrence within the ganglion; they are concentrated more distally and rostrally, approximately from the origin of the palatine ramus to the distal border of the ganglion (g AV+VII; fig.2B).

The three roots of the anteroventral + facial ganglion include a very large dorsolaterally located sensory root, a smaller dorsomedial sensory root, and a single ventral motor root. The fibers of the dorsolateral root have the largest diameter, and these appear to be the central pro-

cesses of the large cells of the combined ganglion. Because of their similarity to the ganglionic cells and processes of the anterodorsal, otic, supratemporal, and posterior lateral line nerves, we regard these cells and this root as the anteroventral lateral line nerve and illustrate this root in blue, in figure 2A (see section on octavolateralis nerves below). This dorsolateral root is the most rostral root of the anteroventral + facial ganglion and it can first be recognized at level RC 720. It joins the ventral root of the anterodorsal lateral line nerve at about level RC 751.

The smaller dorsomedial sensory root of the anteroventral + facial ganglion consists of smaller diameter fibers and runs parallel to the dorsolateral root. At level RC 751, the dorsomedial root turns dorsally to occupy a position between the dorsal root of the anterodorsal nerve and the combined ventral root of the anterodorsal lateral line nerve and the dorsolateral root of the anteroventral + facial ganglion (approximately level RC 791). Because this occurs in the middle of the gap, where we only have every 10th section, we have checked these details against the available series of sections of adults. In the adult, it is clear that the dorsomedial root consists of four or five fascicles which could be mistaken for the entering fibers of the combined ventral root of the anterodorsal and dorsolateral root of the combined anteroventral + facial ganglion. The fibers of the entering dorsomedial root of the anteroventral + facial ganglion, however, pass entirely through the medial octavolateralis nucleus before turning caudally in association with the secondary visceral tract. Most of these fibers probably terminate in the visceral sensory column.

The peripheral distribution of the rami of the facial nerve to the skin of the operculum and hyoid arch indicates that there must be somatosensory fibers in its ganglion and roots. The presence of these fibers is indicated by green in figure 2B. We are unable, however, to distinguish these ganglion cells or their central processes from those of the visceral sensory fibers.

The ventral motor root of the facial nerve exits the medulla at level RC 781. The ventral root is sandwiched between the dorsally entering combined sensory roots of the three preotic lateral line nerves and the ventrally entering octaval nerve (fig.2B). It passes rostrally, ventral to the fused ventral root of the anterodorsal lateral line nerve and the dorsolateral root of the combined anteroventral + facial ganglion (level RC 771), and it enters the caudal pole of the combined ganglion at level RC 761.

The first ramus to arise from the ganglion is the palatine ramus at approximately level RC 700 (pal; fig.2). It appears to consist of only visceral sensory fibers and courses rostrally and ventrally to reach the palate. Its course lies ventral to the jugular vein and on the dorsolateral surface of the prootic cartilage. The ramus continues ventrally until, by level RC 600, it can be seen lateral to the anterior process of the prootic cartilage (a pro; fig. 8). Between this level and level RC 452, the palatine ramus lies in the palate just lateral to the basicranial muscle (bcm; fig. 7), just medial to the opening of the spiracular chamber (spc; fig. 7), and just dorsal to the medial ramule of the pharyngeal ramus of the glossopharyngeal nerve (mp IX; fig. 7; the course of mp IX is truncated in the reconstruction in fig. 2B). The first recognizable ramule of the palatine ramus is at about level RC 285 (lpal 1; fig. 2B). This is a small ramule, approximately one-third of the diameter of the main ramus, which innervates the palatal mucosa medial to the palatoquadrate cartilage (e.g. level RC 260).

The palatine ramus can be traced rostrally in connective tissue adjacent to the mucosa and medial to the palatoquadrate cartilage (pal; fig. 6), until level RC 226 where it divides into medial and lateral ramules (mpal, lpal 2; fig. 2B, 5). The medial ramule passes toward the midline of the palate and comes to lie adjacent to the parasphenoid bone; at level RC 165, it divides into medial and lateral elements (fig. 2B; both of these elements are designated mpal on fig. 4). These elements subsequently ramify in the mucosa anterior to the parasphenoid bone. The lateral ramule of the palatine ramus turns laterally and ventrally to lie adjacent to the medial angle of the palatoquadrate cartilage (lpal 2; fig. 5) where it ramifies in the mucosa and associated connective tissues ventral to the palatoquadrate cartilage (e.g. level RC 100).

The remaining three rami of the facial nerve arise from the hyomandibular trunk (hym; fig. 2A) between levels RC 761 and RC 771. The hyomandibular trunk passes caudally and ventrally through the otico-occipital cartilage dorsal to the ear and ventral to the jugular vein (e.g. level RC 741). Between levels RC 761 and RC 771, it passes into its canal in the hyomandibular cartilage. At this level (level RC 761), the hyomandibular trunk issues two rami that turn rostrally: a dorsolaterally positioned mandibular ramus of the anteroventral lateral line nerve (mAV, described in the section on octavolateralis nerves, below) and a more ventromedially positioned mandibular ramus of the facial nerve (m VII; fig. 2A).

The mandibular ramus of the facial nerve appears to comprise only visceral sensory fibers. It passes rostrally around the lateral surface of the hyomandibular cartilage and continues ventrally at a steep angle along the inner surface of the symplectic cartilage (e.g. level RC 741); by level RC 730, it divides into dorsal and ventral ramules (vm, dm; fig. 2B, 7). The dorsal ramule continues rostrally in the connective tissue of the hyoid arch, immediately dorsal to the hyomandibular cartilage. The surface of the hyoid arch in this region bears many small patches of teeth, and the dorsal ramule can be seen just dorsal and lateral to these tooth patches (dm; fig. 9). The dorsal ramule maintains its position dorsal to the ceratohyal as it courses rostrally (dm; fig. 8, 7) and can be traced about as far forward as level RC 325 (fig. 2B). As it is traced forward, the ramule does not obviously subdivide, but it does decrease in diameter, indicating that it must be innervating the dorsal mucosa and connective tissues of the hyoid arch.

The ventral ramule of the mandibular ramus of the hyomandibular trunk (vm; fig. 2) passes ventrally along the lateral edge of the ceratohyal cartilage and comes to lie on the medial surface of the symplectic cartilage (e.g. level RC 725). From this position, it passes still further ventral and onto the lower jaw where it moves ventrally around the prearticular bone to lie along the ventromedial edge of Meckel's cartilage (vm; fig. 2, 8). The ventral ramule courses rostrally in this position but subsequently courses dorsally and comes to lie adjacent to the medial surface of Meckel's cartilage (vm; fig. 7). At level RC 375, the ramule divides into dorsal and ventral elements which pass as far as the dorsomedial corner of Meckel's cartilage (vm; fig. 6) and terminate by level RC 275. These observations suggest that the ramule mainly innervates the mucosa and associated connective tissues of the medial surface of the jaw.

We now return to the hyoid ramus, which is the next ramus in the series to arise from the hyomandibular trunk (hy; fig. 2B). Unlike the palatine or the mandibular rami, the hyoid ramus contains both sensory and motor elements. It leaves the hyomandibular trunk on a caudal and lateral trajectory and exits the ventrocaudal corner of the hyomandibular cartilage through its own foramen. The position of the ramus with respect to the hyomandibular cartilage can be seen clearly in the transverse section at level RC 820 (note the portion of hy directly ventral to hyo; fig. 10). The ramus continues caudally and ventrally, making a steep bow as it passes anterior to the leading edge of the opercular cartilage. Either three or four ramules issue from the caudal edge of the ramus in this portion of its course; we cannot be certain of the precise number or path of these ramules because they issue during the nearly vertical descent of the hyoid ramus and because this occurs in the area of the gap in sections (three unlabeled ramules are indicated on our reconstruction in fig. 2B; for coverage of the ramules of the hyoid ramus, see Millot and Anthony, 1965, fig. 26). It is clear, however, that these caudally directed ramules innervate the opercular flap and associated muscles. On completing its caudal and ventral descent by level RC 820, the hyoid ramus lies ventral to the caudal end of the ceratohyal cartilage (note portion of hy directly ventral to cer in fig. 10).

From approximately levels RC 770 to RC 781, a ramule passes ventrally from the hyoid ramus to innervate the geniohyoid muscle; this ramule is shown in red but not labeled in the reconstruction (fig. 2B). Tracing rostrally, the hyoid ramus is visible lateral to the geniohyoid muscle (hy; fig. 9). The hyoid ramus remains in this position and continues to issue small ramules to the geniohyoid muscle as it passes forward (hy; fig. 8). At about level RC 530, the ramus issues a larger ramule that passes ventrally and medially to supply the posterior intermandibular muscle; this ramus is shown in red but not labeled on the reconstruction (fig. 2B). The relationships of the hyoid ramus to the genio-hyoid muscle, the posterior intermandibular muscle and the gular plate are shown in the diagram of section RC 452 (hy, gh, imp gup; fig. 7). By level RC 346, the hyoid ramus lies ventral to the posterior intermandibular muscle, and continues to give off additional ramules into the muscle. By level RC 240, the hyoid ramus fuses with the ventral ramule of the mandibular ramus of the trigeminal nerve (v-man+hy; fig. 2B). The combined bundle can be traced as far rostrally as level RC 175 (v-man+hy; fig. 5). To summarize, the hyoid ramus innervates the lateral surface of the opercular region, the muscles of the hyoid arch, and the overlying skin and gular plate in the gular region.

The opercular ramus (or; fig. 2A) is the most caudally and medially directed ramus of the hyomandibular trunk and clearly contains both motor and sensory fibers. It arises between levels RC 781 and RC 791 and immediately thereafter issues a small ventromedially directed ramule (indicated but not labeled in fig. 2A) to supply the hyomandibular adductor muscle (ahm; fig. 10). As the opercular ramus passes caudally, it divides into medial and lateral ramules at level RC 810 (mor, lor; fig. 2A, 10). As the medial ramule continues caudally, it gives rise to a number of small branches which continue to innervate the hyomandibular adductor muscle. At level RC 920, the medial ramule divides into a large medially directed element which anastomoses with the supratemporal and middle lateral line nerves (fig. 2A) and numerous smaller divisions that innervate the opercular adductor muscle and associated skin. We could not trace the caudal terminations of these divisions because this occurs at the end of Block B.

The lateral ramule of the opercular ramus (lor; fig. 2A) exhibits a similar relationship to the opercular muscles and the skin, but there is no evidence of an anastomosis with the supratemporal lateral line nerve. As it is traced caudally, the lateral ramule subdivides into medial and lateral elements, each of which gives rise to a number of divisions which appear to innervate the muscle and adjacent skin.

Octavolateralis Nerves

There is anatomical evidence that six lateral line nerves exist in *Latimeria* in addition to the octaval nerve. The evidence is the presence of six distinctly separate sensory ganglia of these nerves as well as the separate courses of their peripheral rami. Three of these nerves (anterodorsal, anteroventral and otic lateral line nerves) are rostral to the inner ear. The remaining three nerves (middle, supratemporal, and posterior lateral line nerves) originate and distribute caudal to the inner ear.

Anterodorsal Lateral Line Nerve

The sensory ganglion of the anterodorsal lateral line nerve is completely intracranial in the pup. The rostral pole of the ganglion is at level RC 678, lateral to the trigeminal ganglion and ventral to the auricular leaf of the cerebellum (g AD; fig. 2A, 9, 14C). The ganglion extends caudally to level RC 761 and is separated from the trigeminal nerve and ganglion except at its rostral pole. For a distance of approximately 500 microns at the pole (levels RC 676 to RC 695) there is a complex exchange of fibers among the trigeminal, anterodorsal and otic nerves. At this level connective tissue sheaths encapsulating the trigeminal and anterodorsal ganglia are disrupted, and a few trigeminal fibers appear to enter the forming superficial ophthalmic and buccal rami of the anterodorsal lateral line nerve. More importantly, a sizable fascicle of trigeminal fibers arises from the dorsolateral portion of the trigeminal ganglion and enters the dorsal portion of the anterodorsal ganglion, where the trigeminal fibers then move laterally and exit ventrolaterally to fuse with the anterior ramus of the otic nerve. Because the trigeminal fibers actually penetrate the anterodorsal ganglion, there is no simple way to diagram this in our reconstruction.

Immediately rostral to the anterior end of the anterodorsal ganglion, its peripherally coursing fibers divide into two large rami: a dorsally directed superficial ophthalmic ramus and a ventrally coursing buccal ramus (so, buc; fig. 2A, 8, 14A). Immediately caudal to the ganglion, the centrally coursing processes of the sensory cells divide into dorsal and ventral roots. These roots course along the lateral surface of the medulla, terminating in the dorsal and medial octavolateralis nuclei, respectively, between levels RC 775 to RC 810. The dorsal root of the anterodorsal lateral line nerve is indicated in the reconstruction (dr; fig. 2A).

Five ramules arise from the superficial ophthalmic ramus prior to its exit from the neurocranium. In order to simplify the reconstruction in figure 2, only two ramules are illustrated in sequence: the second ramule of the superficial ophthalmic ramus (ar; fig. 2A, 8; here termed the anterior ramule because we consider it homologous to the anterior ramule of other fishes) and the fifth ramule of the superficial ophthalmic ramus (so 5; fig. 2A). The first ramule of the superficial ophthalmic ramus (not shown) arises from the rostral pole of the anterodorsal lateral line ganglion, just proximal to the origin of the anterior ramule. The third and fourth ramules of the superficial ophthalmic ramus (also not shown) arise, respectively, from the dorsal and ventral surfaces of the superficial ophthalmic ramus immediately distal to the origin of the anterior ramule.

The description of the distal distribution of these five ramules follows. The first ramule arises from the lateral surface of the superficial ophthalmic ramus, at the same level where a laterally directed bundle of fibers arises from the dorsal surface of the trigeminal ganglion (level RC 660; fig. 14A). These trigeminal fibers join the first ramule, which courses dorsally and laterally to pass beneath the ventral edge of the otico-occipital cartilage. It then fuses with the first ramule of the buccal ramus (described below) and appears to terminate in the spongy portion of the intertemporal bone. The second (or anterior) ramule arises from the lateral surface of the superficial ophthalmic ramus at level RC 621 and courses dorsally and laterally to pass beneath the otico-occipital cartilage to enter the intertemporal bone where it innervates the most lateral neuromast of the median canal at level RC 545 (mec; fig. 1B).

The third and fourth ramules arise from the dorsal and ventral surfaces, respectively, of the superficial ophthalmic ramus at level RC 614. Like the more proximal ramules, they course dorsally and laterally beneath the dermal bone and terminate adjacent to the dorsalmost tubule of the infraorbital sensory canal and the fenestra (ioc, llf; fig. 1B) formed by the confluence of the supraorbital, infraorbital, and otic canals (level RC 548).

The fifth ramule of the superficial ophthalmic ramus arises at level RC 593 and, like the more proximal ramules, it courses dorsally and laterally to a position medially adjacent to the anterior ramule, where it penetrates the intertemporal bone to innervate the two more medial neuromasts of the median canal (so5; fig. 2A).

Throughout its intracranial course, the superficial ophthalmic ramus lies dorsal to the intracranial venous sinus (so; fig. 8). At level RC 525, it exits the neurocranium and remains a compact bundle throughout the rest of its course. At level RC 490, the ramus enters the posterior canal for the superficial ophthalmic ramus in the sphenethmoid cartilage. The superficial ophthalmic ramus is indicated inside its posterior canal (so, cson; fig. 7), where it is poised to reemerge into the orbit. Anterior to the orbit (fig. 6), the superficial ophthalmic ramus reenters a canal in the sphenethmoid cartilage known as the anterior canal for the superficial ophthalmic ramus. By level RC 275, the ramus is completely enclosed within this canal; it remains closely associated with a canal system in the ethmoid portion of the sphenethmoid cartilage to the tip of the snout (so; fig. 4, 5).

Beginning at level RC 525, seven laterally directed ramules of the superficial ophthalmic ramus innervate the neuromasts of the supraorbital canal (soc; fig. 1B; these ramules are not shown in the reconstruction). Typically, these ramules arise dorsally or laterally from the ramus, then pass rostrally and adjacent to the ramus for some distance before penetrating the sphenethmoid cartilage and the frontal bone to reach the supraorbital canal.

Perhaps the most interesting feature of the supraorbital ramus in *Latimeria* is its innervation of the sensory epithelium associated with the posterior superior and posterior inferior rostral tubes (roe; fig. 2, 5, 16). This requires a brief description of the configuration of the rostral tubes and their surrounding loose connective tissues, sensory epithelia and cartilages. Essentially, the membranous walls of the rostral tubes are invaginations of the surface epithelium of the snout, so that each tube opens to the exterior and ends medially in a cribriform region that has usually been interpreted as an electrosensory epithelium [Hetherington and Bemis, 1979; Bemis and Hetherington, 1982; Jørgenson, 1991]. The membranous walls of each rostral tube are separated from the cartilaginous walls of the rostral cavity by a relatively thick layer of loose connective tissue; these relationships can best be appreciated at relatively low magnification as in figure 5 [also see fig. 2 in Bemis and Hetherington, 1982]. The crypts of the right and left sides do not come into contact at the midline but are separated by a continuation of the connective tissue that surrounds the rostral tubes and is usually called the rostral sac. At level RC 236, the anterior canal for the superficial ophthalmic ramus becomes confluent with the space enclosed by loose connective tissue so that the superficial ophthalmic ramus lies immediately adjacent to the dorsal membranous wall of the posterior superior rostral tube. At level RC 224, the superficial ophthalmic ramus issues a major, medially directed ramule (diagrammed but not labeled in fig. 2A). This ramule passes medially in the loose connective tissue dorsal to the posterior superior rostral tube, then ramifies into at least four major elements that fan over the surface of the membranous wall. These elements continue into the so-called rostral sac and turn ventrally to terminate in the crypts of the sensory epithelium.

The superficial ophthalmic ramus reenters its cartilaginous canal at level RC 193, and then two dorsolaterally directed ramules are given off into the posterior inferior rostral tube (pit; fig. 2A) at level RC 190. Details of the innervation of the posterior inferior rostral tube by ramules of the superficial ophthalmic ramus are shown in figures 5, 16A and 16B. Two large ramules leave the ventrolateral surface of the superficial ophthalmic ramus at levels RC 190 and 188. The origin of the ramule at level RC 188 can be seen in figure 16A. Both ramules then turn medially and divide into numerous elements which course over the roof and walls of the posterior inferior tube as indicated by arrows in figure 16B. These elements then enter the spongy tissue of the rostral sac (roe; fig. 16B), where they appear to terminate among the putative electroreceptors.

The superficial ophthalmic ramus continues rostrally within its cartilaginous canal, issuing ramules to the neuromasts of the supraorbital sensory canal. Significantly, it does not innervate the cribriform region of the anterior rostral tube, which is instead innervated by branches of the buccal ramus of the anterodorsal lateral line nerve.

The buccal ramus of the anterodorsal lateral line nerve is distinct from the superficial ophthalmic ramus by level RC 670 (buc, so; fig. 14A). The first small ramule arises from the lateral surface of the buccal ramus in a complex area at level RC 656 (not shown on reconstruction). This ramule is soon joined by a fascicle of trigeminal fibers which arises from the lateral surface of the trigeminal ganglion and passes between the superficial ophthalmic and buccal rami to anastomose with it. After this, the ramule ascends dorsally and laterally, passes beneath the ventral edge of the otico-occipital cartilage, then fuses with the first ramule of the superficial ophthalmic ramus (described above). The fused ramules then appear to terminate in the spongy portion of the intertemporal bone.

At level RC 625, the buccal ramus and the trigeminal trunk are closely associated, and they exit together through the ventrolateral floor of the neurocranium at the level of the intracranial joint (buc, t V; fig. 8, 15A). Here, a second ramule arises from the dorsal surface of the buccal ramus (b2; fig. 2A) and divides into rostral and caudal elements. The caudally directed element courses dorsally to innervate the skin in association with the first two ramules of the

superficial ophthalmic ramus; the larger rostrally directed element innervates the dermis surrounding the posterior wall of the fenestra of the lateral line (llf; fig. 1B). A third ramule (b3; fig. 2A) arises dorsally from the buccal ramus at level RC 600 and courses laterally to innervate the skin of the anterior wall of the fenestra of the lateral line system formed by the confluence of supraorbital, infraorbital and otic canals. At level RC 595, a dorsomedial segment of the trigeminal trunk diverges to anastomose with the buccal ramus of the anterodorsal lateral line nerve at level RC 575 (see section on trigeminal nerve, above). From this point rostrally, the maxillary ramus of the trigeminal nerve and the buccal ramus of the anterodorsal lateral line nerve form a single complex bundle (buc + max; fig. 2A), while the remaining fibers of the trigeminal trunk constitute the mandibular ramus of the trigeminal nerve (m V; fig. 2). By definition, those fibers of the buccal + maxillary complex that innervate neuromasts derive from the buccal ramus of the anterodorsal lateral line nerve, whereas those that innervate skin or muscle are fibers of the maxillary ramus of the trigeminal nerve as reflected by the blue and green colors of the complex in figure 2.

As the buccal + maxillary complex passes rostrally and ventrally along the dorsolateral border of the mandibular adductor muscle, the fourth and fifth ramules of the buccal ramus arise near level RC 575 (b4, b5; fig. 2A). These ventrally directed ramules repeatedly subdivide and innervate all neuromasts in the caudal part of the infraorbital sensory canal as well as those of the preopercular canal in the cheek (ioc, poc; fig. 1B). Between levels RC 550 and RC 525, the buccal + maxillary complex courses ventrally and medially along the lateral edge of the mandibular adductor muscle to occupy a position ventral to the eye (buc + max; fig. 2A, 6, 7). Between levels RC 525 and RC 240, a number of laterally directed ramules arise to innervate neuromasts in the portion of the infraorbital canal located immediately ventral to the orbit. In addition, at least one ramule arises at level RC 350 to innervate the skin of the angle of the jaw. These and remaining ramules that innervate neuromasts are not indicated on the reconstruction. As the buccal + maxillary complex passes rostral to the orbit, it lies lateral to the palatoquadrate cartilage. It soon divides into lateral and medial ramules, which are initially enclosed in a single encapsulating sheath but subsequently diverge. They can be seen lying lateral to the palatoquadrate cartilage (pq, lr, mr; fig. 2A, 5), and they ramify in a complex manner to innervate the snout.

The medial ramule of the buccal + maxillary complex begins to diverge from the lateral ramule by level RC 205 and divides into dorsal and ventral elements (both labeled mr in fig.5; the elements are not indicated in the reconstruction in fig.2 because of their complexity). At level RC 167, the dorsal element of the medial ramule of the buccal + maxillary complex subdivides into dorsal and ventral divisions. The dorsal division enters the ethmoid portion of the sphenethmoid cartilage lateral to the olfactory bulb. At this same level, the ventral element of the medial ramule also subdivides into dorsal and ventral divisions. At level RC 150, the dorsal division of the dorsal element of the medial ramule enters the olfactory capsule to lie immediately lateral to the olfactory epithelium. The dorsal division of the dorsal element of the medial ramule continues rostrally to lie immediately ventral to the anterior naris in the connective tissue of the olfactory capsule (mr; fig.4). There is no noticeable decrease in the size of the dorsal division as it passes through the olfactory chamber; if it innervates the olfactory organ, it must do so sparsely. At level RC 46, the dorsal division of the dorsal element of the medial ramule enters the ethmoid cartilage, ventral to the rostral pole of the olfactory organ, and courses towards the anterior rostral tube. At levels RC 36 to RC 32, the dorsal division finally branches, and both branches terminate in the connective tissue of the upper lip. The ventral division of the dorsal element of the medial ramule lies dorsal to the lateral ramule and lateral to the ethmoid cartilage. The dorsal and ventral divisions of the ventral element of the medial ramule lie close together in the loose connective tissue ventral to the lateral ramule and immediately dorsal to the lip fold. At level RC 141, the ventral division of the ventral element of the medial ramule enters the connective tissue of the upper lip fold and branches repeatedly before terminating in the fold (the upper lip fold, dlf, is indicated in fig.4, 5). At this same level, both the dorsal division of the ventral element of the medial ramule and the ventral division of the dorsal element of the medial ramule, form dorsal and ventral branches. At level RC 122, branches of the ventral division of the ventral element of the medial ramule also enter the connective tissue of the upper lip fold. The branches of the ventral division of the dorsal element of the medial ramule are closely associated with the cartilage of the olfactory capsule and appear to enter the loose connective tissue between the olfactory organ and the cartilaginous olfactory capsule. The remaining branches of the ventral division of the ventral element of the medial ramule innervate the upper lip fold at this level.

The lateral ramule of the buccal + maxillary complex can be traced forward from level RC 205 (lr; fig.2A). Between levels RC 205 and RC 100, the lateral ramule gives rise to a number of dorsolaterally directed elements that innervate neuromasts of the rostral portion of the infraorbi-

tal canal (lr; fig.5). Initially, the lateral ramule lies on the outer surface of the cartilaginous olfactory capsule; slightly more rostrally, it lies within the capsule (lr; fig.4), then passes ventral to the anterior naris at about level RC 50, and finally enters the cartilage to pass immediately beneath the anterior rostral tube at level RC 41. Between levels RC 40 and RC 25, two very large medially directed elements pass across the ventral floor of the anterior rostral tube (fig.2A, 16C) to innervate the crypts of the rostral sac associated with this tube. A greatly diminished lateral ramule continues in the connective tissue above the roof of the anterior rostral tube to innervate the most rostral neuromasts at the tip of the snout.

Given the pattern of innervation of the fibers of the lateral ramule of the buccal + maxillary complex versus that of the medial ramule, it is clear that the lateral ramus consists primarily, if not exclusively, of fibers derived from the buccal ramus of the anterodorsal lateral line nerve, whereas fibers of the medial ramule are exclusively derived from the maxillary ramus of the trigeminal nerve. It is equally clear that the sensory epithelia of the rostral organ are separately innervated by the two rami (superficial ophthalmic and buccal) of the anterodorsal lateral line nerve.

Anteroventral Lateral Line Nerve

Traditionally, the ramus that innervates the neuromasts of the preopercular and mandibular sensory canals (mac, poc; fig.1B) has been interpreted as a ramus of the facial nerve, usually termed the external mandibular ramus [e.g. Norris, 1925]. The extensive literature on the development of the lateral line receptors and their associated nerves, however, reflects the separate origin of these lateral line components from placodes located on the dorsolateral surface of the embryonic head [see reviews by Northcutt, 1989, 1990, 1992a]. The results of these studies indicate that each dorsolateral placode that gives rise to neuromasts also gives rise to a cranial nerve which innervates these receptors and remains distinct from all other cranial nerves, even in the adult stage. The key exception to this pattern is the ganglion arising from the dorsolateral placode located on the cheek that gives rise to the preopercular and mandibular lines. The ganglion derived from this placode is initially separate from the facial ganglion, which is derived from neural crest and an epibranchial placode. During subsequent development, however, the two ganglia may become juxtaposed [elasmobranchs; Landacre, 1916] or even fused [amphibians; Coghill, 1916]. Based on this comparative embryological evidence, we regard the ramus that innervates the preopercular and mandibular lines, together with its ganglion cells and its root as a distinct cranial nerve.

Latimeria provides strong support for this interpretation. First, the ganglion clearly consists of two distinct populations of sensory neurons (g AV+VII; fig.14B, D). Dorsally, the cells of the ganglion are very large, palely staining, and identical in appearance to the ganglionic cells of most of the other lateral line nerves. In contrast, the more ventral sensory neurons of the ganglion are smaller, more darkly staining, and identical to ganglionic cells of the nerves traditionally recognized as branchiomeric nerves. Secondly, the centrally directed neurites of the large, palely staining ganglionic cells, which we believe innervate the neuromasts of the mandibular sensory line, join the ventral root of the anterodorsal lateral line nerve together with fibers of the otic lateral line nerve. More centrally, fibers from all three of these preotic lateral line nerves enter the medial octavolateralis nucleus, which is known to be the primary sensory nucleus associated with mechanoreceptive information from neuromasts [Bodznick and Northcutt, 1980; Song and Northcutt, 1991a, b]. Without the availability of early embryological material (currently unknown for *Latimeria*), these two features are the only basis for recognizing the existence of a separate anteroventral lateral line nerve in *Latimeria*.

The large, dorsally located, palely staining cells of the anteroventral + facial ganglion extend the entire distance plotted for the ganglion in figure 2A. Approximately the medial half of the ganglion lies within its canal in the prootic cartilage (g AV+VII; fig.14B). More laterally, the ganglion is topographically outside the neurocranium (g AV+VII; fig.9). The centrally directed processes of the cells that we interpret as the anteroventral nerve course dorsally and caudally, passing ventral and caudal to the ganglia of the anterodorsal and otic lateral line nerves (level RC 720) and subsequently fusing with the ventral root of the anterodorsal lateral line nerve at level RC 671.

The peripherally coursing processes of the ganglion cells of the anteroventral lateral line nerve pass laterally and caudally in the hyomandibular trunk (hym; fig.2B). The trunk enters a canal in the hyomandibular cartilage at level RC 771, where it gives rise to the four major rami noted in the section on the facial nerve (above). In this section, we need to trace the only one of these rami carrying lateralis fibers, which we term the mandibular ramus of the anteroventral nerve (m AV; fig.2A). This ramus lies within the hyomandibular canal, immediately lateral to the mandibular ramus of the facial nerve (m AV, m VII, level RC 775; fig.2A). It hooks sharply rostrally and ventrally, passing

along the wall of the operculum, lateral to the symplectic cartilage, to eventually reach the lower jaw. Its course is very steep in this region, and several cross sections of the nerve are sometimes apparent, as in figure 9 (m AV). Small ramules leave the ramus and pass ventrally and caudally to innervate the neuromasts of the subopercular canal (soc; fig.1B). The main ramus continues to move ventrally, eventually becoming closely associated with the lateral face of Meckel's cartilage (m AV; fig.8), even occupying a groove in the cartilage more rostrally (fig.5). Throughout its course to the tip of the lower jaw, the mandibular ramus of the anteroventral lateral line nerve parallels the mandibular sensory canal (mac; fig.1B) and issues ramules laterally to innervate the neuromasts of this canal.

Otic Lateral Line Nerve

Traditionally, the ramus that innervates the neuromasts of the otic sensory canal (otc; fig.1B) and the neuromast-like organs of the spiracular cavity (if present) has been interpreted as a ramus of the facial nerve [Norris and Hughes, 1920]. In *Latimeria*, however, the fibers that innervate these organs possess a distinct sensory ganglion and root that is completely separate from the facial nerve. For these two reasons we recognize this ganglion and its peripheral processes as a distinct cranial nerve, which we term the otic lateral line nerve.

The sensory ganglion of the otic lateral line nerve is located intracranially, rostral and dorsal to the fused anteroventral + facial ganglion and immediately ventral to the sensory ganglion of the anterodorsal lateral line nerve. The otic ganglion is a compact ovoid located between levels RC 708 and RC 720 (g O; fig.2A). Its cells are large and palely stained, like those of most other lateral line ganglia. The caudal pole of the otic ganglion lies immediately adjacent to, and may be fused with, the posteroventral pole of the ganglion of the anterodorsal lateral line nerve (level RC 751); a short caudally and dorsally directed root of the otic ganglion merges with the ventral root of the anterodorsal nerve prior to the latter's fusion with the root of the anteroventral lateral line nerve.

Peripherally coursing fibers of the ganglionic cells of the otic lateral line nerve form rostrally and posterolaterally directed rami (a O, p O; fig.2A). The anterior ramus issues from the rostral pole of the otic ganglion and passes rostrally a short distance within the cranium (fig.14C), immediately dorsal to the ventrolateral intracranial venous sinus (level RC 680). At level RC 655, it passes from the cranium into the intertemporal bone where it innervates the most rostral neuromast of the otic canal, located between levels RC 600 and RC 625.

The posterior ramus of the otic nerve (p O; fig.2A) arises from the ventral surface of the otic ganglion and passes laterally over the entering root of the facial nerve (p O; fig.14B). The ramus moves dorsolaterally to pass through a separate canal in the otico-occipital cartilage dorsal to the exit of the facial nerve (note the lateral location of p O in fig.14B). As the posterior ramus approaches the neurocranial wall, however, it issues a ramule which passes over the dorsal surface of the facial nerve and accompanies the facial nerve as it emerges from the braincase (levels RC 715 through RC 705). Subsequently this ramule of the posterior ramus of the otic nerve turns rostrally to run ventral to the jugular vein (level RC 695) and courses ventrolaterally in the connective tissue immediately adjacent to the medial wall of the spiracular chamber (spc; fig.3; sr; fig.2A). This ramule cannot be followed rostral to level RC 670, we assume it ramifies in the connective tissue in the wall of the spiracular chamber.

It is possible that this ramus also innervates one or more spiracular organs, although it is unclear from our study whether *Latimeria* possesses spiracular sense organs. The spiracular chamber is large (spc; fig.3). It opens into the pharynx between levels RC 600 and RC 725 (fig.3, 7–9). Rostrally, the roof and medial wall of the chamber lie lateral to the basicranial joint (e.g. level RC 614). Slightly more caudally, between levels RC 627 and RC 675, the dorsalmost portion of the spiracular chamber is separated by only a thin layer of connective tissue from the lateral line canal fenestra formed by the confluence of the otic, supraorbital, and infraorbital sensory canals (llf; fig.1B). More caudally (level RC 686), there are two hillock-like thickenings in the dermis of the lateral wall of the chamber that may be the dermal bases of spiracular organs. We cannot recognize hair cells in the epithelium overlying these dermal bases, but the internal surface of the chamber is poorly preserved in the pup, so we cannot rule out their existence. In other anamniotes, spiracular organs are innervated by an anterior ramule of the otic lateral line nerve [Norris and Hughes, 1920; Norris, 1925], but we were unable to trace the ramule of the posterior ramus of the otic lateral line (sr; fig.2A) to these hillocks. As additional specimens become available, this area should be examined closely to determine whether spiracular organs exist. More caudally (level RC 725), the spiracular chamber lies dorsal to the hyomandibular cartilage and is separated from the preopercular canal by only a thin layer of dermis; these relationships are especially apparent in figure 9 (spc). Thus, the caudal end of the spiracular chamber effectively enwraps the hyomandibular cartilage and surrounds the dorsolateral surface of the otic capsule.

Next we trace the continued course of the posterior ramus of the otic lateral line nerve (p O; fig.2A). After emerging from the wall of the braincase (p O; fig.14B), the posterior ramus of the otic nerve turns caudally to run along the lateral surface of the otico-occipital cartilage (p O; fig.9). Between levels RC 725 and RC 750, a second ramule arises from the posterior ramus and passes dorsolaterally and rostrally to innervate the second neuromast of the otic sensory canal between levels RC 675 and RC 700 (o2; fig.2A). As the posterior ramus of the otic nerve continues caudally, it passes through a foramen in the neurocranium (level RC 751) just dorsal to the cartilaginous labyrinth of the ear, and re-emerges at level RC 781, where a third ramule arises, passing laterally and dorsally to innervate the third through the fifth neuromasts of the otic canal (o3; fig.2A; neuromasts are between levels RC 700 and RC 825). The remaining fibers of the posterior ramus of the otic nerve continue to run adjacent to the dorsolateral surface of the neurocranium, where they anastomose with the middle lateral line nerve and the ventral ramus of the supratemporal lateral line nerve between levels RC 925 and RC 950; we therefore term this last portion of the otic nerve the otic commissure (oc; fig.2A, 10) and indicate it in green because we interpret that it carries fibers from either the trigeminal or facial nerve to innervate the skin of this region (see Discussion).

Octaval Nerve

Much of the inner ear and octaval nerve in the pup lie within the gap, the area for which only every 10th section is available; fine details are therefore difficult to reconstruct. It has been possible to reconstruct the membranous labyrinth as outlined in figure 3 (sac, hscc, pscc), but only general details of the octaval nerve are presented here.

The ganglion of the octaval nerve is completely intracranial. Its cells extend medially from the neurocranial wall to within a short distance of the entry of its very short roots into the medulla. The roots enter the medulla between levels RC 781 and RC 791, immediately ventral to the motor root of the facial nerve and the still more dorsally lying roots of the three preotic lateral line nerves (VIII; fig.2).

The peripheral processes of the octaval nerve form a short trunk and, on emerging into the cavity of the inner ear, divide into anterior and posterior rami (not shown). The anterior ramus innervates the maculae of the utricle and the anterior semicircular canal. The posterior ramus innervates the remaining maculae of the inner ear. Sections through elements of this posterior ramule can be seen medial to the saccule in level RC 820 (sac, VIII; fig. 10).

Middle Lateral Line Nerve

Historically, the glossopharyngeal nerve has been claimed to include a ramus that innervates neuromasts of the temporal sensory canal and the middle pit line [Allis, 1897; Norris and Hughes, 1920; Norris, 1925]. A recent study of gars [Song and Northcutt, 1991a], however, has demonstrated that a separate lateral line nerve, which is closely associate with the glossopharyngeal nerve but distinct from it, is responsible for innervating neuromasts of the middle pit line and temporal canal. This nerve has been termed the middle lateral line nerve, and the pattern seen in *Latimeria* conforms to that seen in gars (MLLN; fig. 2A).

The ganglion of the middle lateral line nerve spans levels RC 898 through RC 908 and lies dorsal and medial to the lateral ganglion of the glossopharyngeal nerve (g MLLN; fig. 2A, 17A). Its cells are palely staining like those of the other lateral line nerves, but they do not appear to be as large and they are few in number. The root of the middle lateral line nerve courses medially through the glossopharyngeal foramen in the cartilage of the postotic process; on emerging into the cranium, it passes caudally and dorsally to fuse with the roots of the other postotic lateral line nerves (fig. 2A) at level RC 845.

A single ramus emerges from the posterodorsal border of the middle lateral line ganglion (g MLLN; fig. 2A), passes around the medial surface of the jugular vein, and continues dorsally along the edge of the postotic process of the otico-occipital cartilage. After passing through its own small foramen in the postotic process (r ML; fig. 11), the ramus fuses almost immediately with the ventral ramus of the supratemporal lateral line nerve (v ST; fig. 2A). Due to this anastomosis, it is impossible to determine which neuromasts are innervated by the middle lateral line nerve in *Latimeria*. It is possible, however, that this nerve innervates neuromasts of both the temporal canal (tc; fig. 1B) and the middle pit line.

In this region in other fishes, there are normally middle and posterior pit lines [as in gars; see Song and Northcutt, 1991a]. Millot and Anthony [1958, plate XIX] identified two pit lines in this region, whereas Hensel [1986] recognized pit organs forming lines in an inverted-Y pattern, in which he named each branch of the Y as a separate pit line. In other fishes, however, the important criterion for distinguishing middle and posterior pit lines is their innervation by the middle and supratemporal lateral line nerves, respectively. Since these two nerves anastomose in *Latimeria*, either or both nerves could be innervating the pit lines indicated by these previous authors.

Supratemporal Lateral Line Nerve

In classical accounts [e.g. Norris, 1925] the first ramus to arise from the posterior lateral line nerve is termed the supratemporal ramus, and it innervates neuromasts of the posttemporal and supratemporal canals as well as the neuromasts of the posterior pit line. In gars and other basal actinopterygian fishes, those ganglionic cells whose peripheral processes constitute this supratemporal ramus lie within a distinct mediodorsal subdivision of the posterior lateral line ganglion [Song and Northcutt, 1991a]. The subpopulation of ganglion cells that gives rise to the supratemporal ramus is more distinct in *Latimeria* than in gars. Also, there is descriptive embryological evidence [Landacre and Conger, 1913; Landacre, 1916; Stone, 1922; see Northcutt, 1992a for review] that this population of ganglion cells arises from a dorsolateral placode distinct from the placode that gives rise to the posterior lateral line nerve. These two facts cause us to interpret the supratemporal ganglion and its rami as a distinct cranial nerve which we term the supratemporal lateral line nerve.

The ganglion of the supratemporal lateral line nerve is entirely intracranial. It rostral border lies dorsal and medial to the ganglion of the posterior lateral line nerve (g ST, g PLLN; fig. 2A, 17C). Throughout their extent, the ganglia of the supratemporal lateral line nerve and the underlying posterior lateral line nerve are clearly separated by sheaths of connective tissue. The ganglion cells of the supratemporal lateral line nerve are large and palely stained like those of the other lateral line ganglia. The root of the supratemporal nerve fuses with the root of the posterior lateral line nerve at level RC 938 (fig. 2A, 17C). These relationships are clearly seen between levels RC 935 and RC 940. After joining with the root of the middle lateral line nerve, the common root of all three postotic lateral line nerves (r POL; fig. 2A) enters the medulla at levels RC 825–840.

The peripherally directed fibers of the supratemporal ganglion travel laterally and ventrally in a short trunk into the vagal foramen, together with the posterior lateral line ganglion and vagal trunk (st, PLLN, t X; fig. 17B). Within the vagal foramen, the supratemporal trunk divides into dorsal and ventral rami. The dorsal ramus turns dorsally, then crosses rostrally over the ventral ramus (d ST, v ST; fig. 2A) and courses laterally along the outer surface of the otico-occipital cartilage (d ST; fig. 11), subsequently anastomosing with a more distally arising anterior ramule of the ventral ramus of the supratemporal lateral line nerve (a ST; fig. 2A, 11). This anastomosis occurs at about level RC 875; rostral to this level, the combined bundle courses rostrally along the external surface of the neurocranium and divides into medial and lateral elements (unlabeled split at level RC 800) to innervate the neuromasts of the supratemporal canal (STC; fig. 1B).

We return to trace the ventral ramus of the supratemporal lateral line nerve lateral to the origin of its anterior ramule (v ST; fig. 2A). The ramus continues laterally and first issues a caudolaterally directed ramule to innervate the most caudal neuromast of the posttemporal canal at the level of RC 950 (shown but not labeled on fig. 2A). Shortly thereafter, the ramus forms a complex anastomosis with the middle lateral line ramus (shown but not labeled on fig. 2A), the otic commissure (oc; fig. 2A), and an element of the medial ramule of the opercular ramus of the facial nerve (shown but not labeled in fig. 2A). One additional ramule is issued from the point of anastomosis to pass rostrally and laterally to innervate the first neuromast of the posttemporal sensory canal at the level of RC 900 (shown in blue but not labeled in fig. 2A).

Posterior Lateral Line Nerve

Historically, the ganglionic cells and their peripheral processes that innervate the neuromasts of the trunk and tail were interpreted as a component of the vagal nerve [Strong, 1895; Allis, 1897; Norris and Hughes, 1920; Norris, 1925]. All recent studies, however, demonstrate that the cells innervating these neuromasts constitute a distinct ganglion and root, totally separate from the vagal and glossopharyngeal nerves [see review by Northcutt, 1989]. Therefore, we consider that these fibers constitute a separate cranial nerve termed the posterior lateral line nerve.

The rostral pole of the ganglion of the posterior lateral line nerve occurs at level RC 921, where the ganglion lies ventral to the medial ganglion of the vagal nerve and lateral to the vagal trunk (g PLLLN, mg X, t X; fig. 2A, 11, 17B, C, D). The ganglion extends caudally out of the vagal foramen in company with the vagal trunk and the trunk of the supratemporal lateral line nerve, and continues outside the cranium to level RC 979. As in most of the other lateral line ganglia, the cells of the posterior lateral line ganglion are large and palely staining. The root of the posterior lateral line nerve issues from the rostral end of the ganglion and fuses with the root of the supratemporal lateral line

nerve; the combined root courses rostrally and dorsally, laterally adjacent to the vagal trunk, and at level RC 871, it passes dorsal to the rostral pole of the medial ganglion of the vagal nerve and continues rostrally to join the root of the middle lateral line nerve (shown with dashed line near level RC 845; fig. 2A). The combined root of all three postotic lateral line nerves continues rostrally, passing dorsal to the medial ganglion and root of the glossopharyngeal nerve to enter the medial octavolateralis nucleus of the medulla, dorsal to the entering fibers of the glossopharyngeal nerve (between about levels RC 825 and RC 840).

One neuromast ramule and two larger rami arise from the ganglion of the posterior lateral line nerve near its distal terminus. The neuromast ramule (unlabeled in fig. 2A) passes dorsally and laterally to innervate the first neuromast of the trunk canal at approximately level RC 975. What we label as the dorsal ramus (d; fig. 2A) runs dorsally adjacent to the much larger lateral ramus of the posterior lateral line nerve (l PLLN; fig. 2A). The dorsal and lateral rami of the posterior lateral line nerve cannot be followed further caudally in the pup because this is the end of Block B. In other fishes, however, the lateral ramus innervates the neuromasts of the trunk line (ltc; fig. 1B), and this is almost certainly the case in *Latimeria*. The fate of our dorsal ramus is unclear. It might simply be the second ramule of the posterior lateral line nerve, in which case it would innervate the second neuromast of the lateral trunk canal. It is also possible, however, that our dorsal ramus is homologous to the dorsal ramus of the posterior lateral line nerve of other fishes, in which case it would innervate a dorsal line of superficial neuromasts that run a variable length along the trunk [Song and Northcutt, 1991a].

Glossopharyngeal Nerve

In *Latimeria*, the glossopharyngeal nerve has distinct medial and lateral ganglia (mg IX, lg IX; fig. 2B, 18). The most rostral of its three rami is the pharyngeal ramus (p IX; fig. 2B, 18), which is composed of visceral sensory fibers from the middle two-thirds of the palate and pharyngeal roof. Next is the pretrematic ramus, which conveys visceral sensory information from tissues of the hyoidean hemibranch (pr IX, hhb; fig. 2B, 11, 18). Third and most caudal is the posttrematic ramus, which carries both visceral and motor fibers and innervates the structures of the first gill arch (pt IX; fig. 18). The posttrematic ramus splits almost immediately into dorsal and ventral ramules (dr IX, vr IX; fig. 2B, 18).

The two glossopharyngeal ganglia are connected by a trunk (mg IX, t IX, lg IX; fig.2B, 17A). The cells of both glossopharyngeal ganglia are smaller and more darkly stained than are the ganglionic cells of the lateral line nerves and are comparable in size and staining properties to those of the profundal, trigeminal, and vagal nerves. They are also comparable to the ventral cells of the anteroventral + facial ganglion that we interpret as the sensory cells of the facial nerve. The medial ganglion of the glossopharyngeal nerve is housed entirely within the neurocranium, whereas the lateral ganglion lies outside the neurocranium, just ventral to the cartilage of the postotic process (fig.11, 17A). The lateral ganglion is directly ventral to the jugular vein and medial to the first pharyngobranchial cartilage. All fibers of the glossopharyngeal nerve travel in the glossopharyngeal trunk through its foramen in the cartilage of the postotic process. These fibers include the centrally coursing processes of cells located in the lateral ganglion, the peripherally coursing processes of cells located in the medial ganglion, and motor fibers (fig.2B). The sensory and motor fibers of the glossopharyngeal nerve form a single root, which issues from the medial border of the medial ganglion, passes ventral to the combined roots of the postotic lateral line nerves, and enters the medulla immediately ventral to the entering fibers of the combined roots of the postotic lateral line nerves at approximately level RC 820 (r POL; r IX; fig.2A, 10).

We now describe the rami of the glossopharyngeal nerve. At level RC 890, the posttrematic ramus arises from the dorsolateral surface of the lateral ganglion (pt IX; fig.18; this short ramus is shown but not labeled on fig.2B). The pharyngeal and pretrematic rami originate from the ventrolateral surface of the lateral ganglion as a common trunk, immediately ventral and medial to the origin of the posttrematic ramus. This trunk continues rostrally and divides into pharyngeal and pretrematic rami at level RC 875 (p IX, pr IX; fig.2B, 18). The pretrematic ramus courses laterally (pr IX; fig.2B, 10, 18), passes dorsal to the first pharyngobranchial cartilage and anterior to the levator muscle of the first arch, then moves ventrally. The pharyngeal ramus continues rostrally (p IX; fig.2B, 18). It passes ventral to the hyomandibular adductor muscle (ahm; fig.10), where it divides into lateral and medial ramules (lp IX and mp IX; fig.2B, 10). The lateral ramule (lp IX; fig.2B) courses rostrally and passes between epibranchial cartilages of arches 1 and 2 to ramify in the dorsal portion of the mucosa and connective tissue between the first and second gill arches (e.g. levels RC 725 to RC 761). The medial ramule continues rostrally, remaining ventral to the hyomandibular adductor muscle; at level RC 820, it divides into medial and lateral elements (for simplicity, only the medial element of the medial ramule is illustrated in fig.2B as mp IX). The lateral element continues rostrally and ramifies in the mucosa of the palate. The medial element courses medially and rostrally to level RC 675, where it divides into medial and lateral divisions (shown but not labeled on fig.2B); each of these divisions continues rostrally to innervate the palatal mucosa ventral to the basicranial muscle, with the most rostral extent being level RC 380 (mp IX, fig.7–9).

We return now to the distal continuation of the pretrematic ramus of the glossopharyngeal nerve. After passing dorsal to the first pharyngobranchial cartilage, the pretrematic ramus lies just ventral to the hyomandibular adductor muscle (level RC 850). The ramus continues anteriorly and laterally, then turns ventrally to run adjacent to the hyomandibular cartilage (level RC 800); further ventrally and caudally, it enters the hyoidean hemibranch at level RC 845, where it ramifies and extends caudally the length of the hemibranch (pr IX; fig.2B, 18). Thus, this ramus forms a rostral loop to reach the hyoidean hemibranch (pr IX; fig. 18), which is actually located caudal to the origin of the ramus. For this reason, both the dorsal and ventral portions of the loop can be seen in the figure (pr IX; fig. 10; the dorsal portion lies just ventral to the hyomandibular adductor muscle, and the ventral portion is ventral to the hyomandibular cartilage).

As described above, the posttrematic ramus of the glossopharyngeal nerve arises at level RC 890 from the dorsolateral border of the lateral ganglion (pt IX; fig.18). It passes ventral to the jugular vein, dorsal to the first pharyngobranchial cartilage, and immediately divides into a small dorsal ramule and a much larger ventral ramule (dr IX, vr IX; fig. 2B, 18). The dorsal ramule courses rostrally and laterally, passing dorsal to the levator muscle of the first arch, then laterally and ventrally (level RC 859) to enter the connective tissue of the first arch, where it passes along the lateral edge of the first ceratobranchial cartilage (level RC 849). By level RC 810, it has reached a canal on the dorsolateral surface of the first arch, in which it runs rostrally the length of the first gill arch (dr IX; fig.2B, 7–10, 18, 19). From levels RC 791 to RC 740, the dorsal ramule is divided into medial and lateral elements; still further rostrally, these elements fuse.

The much larger ventral ramule of the posttrematic ramus of the glossopharyngeal nerve (vr IX; fig.2B, 18) also passes over the dorsal surface of the levator muscle of the first arch, then continues caudally to pass around the caudal end of the first ceratobranchial cartilage, where it enters the first arch at level RC 917. On entering the arch, the ventral ramule divides into medial and lateral elements (shown but not labeled in fig. 2B); the lateral element soon divides into medial and lateral divisions (md, ld; fig. 18, 19; shown but not labeled in 2B). Also near the level of RC 917, the pretrematic ramus of the vagal nerve enters the posterior corner of the first arch (1 pr X; fig. 2B, 18). This ramus passes ventrally to lie medial to the three fascicles of the ventral ramule of the posttrematic ramus of the glosso-pharyngeal nerve. These fascicles of the glossopharyngeal and vagal nerves then anastomose. The pretrematic ramus of the vagal nerve anastomoses with the medial element of the ventral ramule of the posttrematic ramus of the glosso-pharyngeal nerve (me+1 pr X; fig. 18, 19) and may also contribute fibers to the medial division of the lateral element of the ventral ramule of the posttrematic ramus of the glossopharyngeal nerve. To avoid cluttering the diagrams of the transverse sections, we have abbreviated all of these fibers as 'gp' in these sections (fig. 5–11; see also fig. 22). Rostrally at level RC 262, there is further branching of the medial division; by level RC 227, these branches have moved dorsally and medially to pass between the cerato-branchial cartilage of the first arch and the copular cartilage of the tongue (cb1, ton; fig. 5). These branches terminate in the mucosal surface of the tongue lateral to the copular cartilage near level RC 100.

Vagal Nerve

The vagal nerve consists of medial and lateral ganglia, joined by a long trunk, and a number of rami that innervate the caudal portion of the pharynx, the structures of the second, third, fourth and fifth gills, and the visceral wall caudal to the pharynx (mg X, t X, lg X; fig. 2B). Our description of the branches of the vagal nerve is necessarily incomplete, as the available sections end before the caudal end of the gill arches (fig. 1A, inset). The sections through the second and third gills provide sufficient evidence, however, to recognize and document four basic similarities in organization between the glossopharyngeal and vagal nerves: (1) the presence of medial and lateral ganglia; (2) the occurrence of pharyngeal rami that innervate the mucosa of the roof of the pharynx; (3) pretrematic rami that pass into each preceding gill arch, and (4) posttrematic rami that divide into dorsal and ventral ramules, innervating the oral and respiratory surfaces of each gill arch, respectively.

The medial ganglion of the vagal nerve is entirely intra-cranial. It begins at level RC 875 and ends at level RC 936 (mg X; fig. 2B). Its origin lies dorsomedial to the entering roots of the postotic lateral line nerves; further caudally, it

is both medial and ventral to the combined roots of the postotic lateral line nerves (r POL; fig. 2A). The vagal trunk passes ventral to those roots to exit the neurocranium (t X; fig. 2, 17C) via the vagal foramen in the otico-occipital cartilage at about level RC 945 (mg X; fig. 2B, 11, 17B, C, D). The lateral ganglion lies dorsolateral to the jugular vein and the second pharyngobranchial cartilage and medial to the levator muscle of the third and fourth gill arches (lg X; fig. 2B, 11, 18). The rostral pole of the lateral ganglion begins at level RC 927; its caudal pole cannot be determined as it is still present at the level of section RC 1005, which is the last intact section on the left side of the specimen (we show the ganglion ending in fig. 2B based on the right side of the pup). The lateral ganglion of the vagal nerve passes caudally and laterally, forming an 'L' shape (lg X; fig. 2B). Enough of the lateral ganglion is intact so that we can recognize rostral and caudal populations of sensory cells, as reported for other fishes [e.g. sharks, Norris and Hughes, 1920; bowfins, gars, sturgeons and paddlefishes, Norris, 1925; gars, Song and Northcutt, 1991a]. The somata of the medial and lateral ganglia consist of small, darkly staining cells similar to those of the other branchio-meric ganglia.

Several roots of the vagal nerve issue from the dorsome-dial border of the medial ganglion (fig. 2B). There is no evidence of separate dorsal sensory and ventral motor roots; rather, these roots constitute a rostral to caudal series entering the wall of the medulla between levels RC 843 and RC 939.

The first pharyngeal ramus and the first pretrematic ramus arise from a common trunk, which emerges from the lateral ganglion at level RC 931 (shown but not labeled on fig. 2B). The origins of this trunk from the lateral ganglion can be seen in figure 11 (lg X; 1p X is shown but not labeled on fig. 2B). At about level RC 903, the common trunk divides into the first pretrematic ramus and the first pharyngeal ramus (1p X, 1pr X; fig. 18). The first pretrematic ramus passes laterally and ventrally around the second pharyngobranchial cartilage, then ventral to the levator muscle of the first gill arch (1 pr X; fig. 18, 19). It loops caudally and enters the first gill arch at level RC 907, and its further course is described in the section on the glossopharyngeal nerve. The first pharyngeal ramus passes medial to the first pharyngobranchial cartilage, then continues rostrally; by about level RC 840, it divides into medial and lateral ramules (m1p X; fig. 2B, 9, 10; l1p X; fig. 2B, 10). The lateral ramule courses rostrolaterally and appears to ramify in the mucosa adjacent to the flap that marks the opening of the spiracular chamber into the pharynx. The medial ramule at level RC 800 lies between the basicranial muscle and second epibranchial cartilage, where it divides into medial and lateral elements. Both elements continue rostrally, and by level RC 761, the medial element divides into medial and lateral divisions. All fascicles arising from the medial ramule innervate the mucosa and connective tissue of the roof of the pharynx as far rostrally as level RC 650.

We now return to the first posttrematic ramus of the vagal nerve (1pt X; fig.2B, 18). It arises from the dorsolateral face of the lateral ganglion at the same level (RC 931) as the trunk of the first pretrematic and first pharyngeal rami. It passes rostrally on the lateral face of the second pharyngobranchial cartilage to about level RC 915 before dividing into dorsal and ventral ramules (dr X, vr X; fig.2B, 18). These ramules then turn caudally and pass around the anterior surface of the second branchial levator muscle (level RC 921), apparently its point of innervation. The dorsal ramule passes caudally along the medial face of the second branchial levator muscle, and enters the second gill arch between levels RC 940 and RC 945 (we have shifted slightly the position of dr X in order to show it in fig.2B). The ventral ramule continues caudally, passes around the caudal border of the second epibranchial cartilage, and enters the base of the second gill arch at about level RC 1000 (vr X; fig.2B, 18).

At level RC 955, the second pharyngeal ramus and the second pretrematic ramus (2p X, 2pr X; fig.2B) originate adjacently from the ventral surface of the lateral ganglion. The second pharyngeal ramus passes ventrally, medial to the second pharyngobranchial cartilage (2p X, pb2; fig.11), to lie lateral to the base of the cranium; at level RC 931, it divides into medial and lateral ramules (indicated but not labeled in fig.2B). As the medial ramule continues forward, it divides into medial and lateral elements at the level of section RC 913, with the lateral element dividing extensively at level RC 899. The lateral ramule supplies the connective tissue and mucosa of the pharyngeal roof, whereas the medial ramule and its subdivisions ramify in the mucosa and connective tissue ventral to the basicranial muscle. There is no evidence that any of these fibers innervate the basicranial muscle as diagrammed by Millot and Anthony [1965; 'nerf sousc', their fig.31].

The second pretrematic ramus of the vagal nerve (2pr X; fig.2B, 18) courses caudally, then turns laterally to pass between the second branchial levator muscle and third and fourth branchial levator muscles. We cannot tell from our specimen whether the third and fourth branchial levators are separate muscles, because the available sections do not extend caudally enough, but in their figure 31, Millot and Anthony [1965] seem to imply that these muscles are fused. Ventral to these levator muscles, the pretrematic ramus issues a ramule which may innervate them (if correct, this is an unusual case of motor fibers being carried in a pretrematic ramus). The remaining portion of the pretrematic ramus continues to course caudally, passing under the pharyngobranchial cartilage of the second arch and on into the second arch (2pr X; fig.18).

The next recognizable vagal ramus arises from the medial edge of the lateral ganglion at the level of section RC 991, but we cannot trace this ramus for any distance, because the sections end shortly thereafter. Comparison with Millot and Anthony [1965, their fig.31, nX br. p. = posterior branch of the vagal nerve] suggests that this ramus may innervate the remaining gill arches, and we have designated it pb X (fig.2B) following their convention. Finally, although the sections end before the caudal end of the lateral ganglion on the left side of the pup, it is obvious that the vagal nerve continues caudally as the visceral ramus.

Occipital Nerves

Three nerve roots arise from the ventral surface of the medulla between the levels RC 900 and RC 1000 (on; fig.2A). There is no trace of corresponding dorsal roots or dorsal root ganglia prior to level RC 975, where the first dorsal root occurs (ds; fig.2A), demarcating the first spinal nerve. Even though we cannot trace the three rostral roots indicated in figure 2A, owing to the end of Block B, they must correspond to the occipital nerves of other anamniotes, which course caudally and ventrally to innervate the hypobranchial muscles of the head. This conclusion is corroborated by Millot and Anthony [1965, their fig. 34], who illustrate three occipital nerves.

Discussion

Our discussion deals with individual cranial nerves in rostral to caudal order. Under the heading for each nerve, we compare our findings with those reported for *Latimeria* by Millot and Anthony [1965], and make phylogenetic comparisons with other craniates to determine whether the particular character states in *Latimeria* are common to all craniates or synapomorphies at some level within craniates. In general, Millot and Anthony [1965] provided clear and usually accurate descriptions of the rami of the cranial nerves, and most of our points of disagreement with them relate to structures that would not have been visible in their gross dissections. Importantly, however, their inability to study the histological organization of the cranial ganglia caused them to misinterpret the components of several nerves. Also, because they lacked a conception of the six lateral line nerves, they made several basic misinterpretations of the preotic and postotic cranial nerves.

Characters of the cranial nerves and ganglia have been used in some phylogenetic systematic studies. For example, the prootic ganglion (a fusion of the trigeminal + facial ganglia [Sokol, 1975]), is apparently a synapomorphy of derived anurans [Duellman and Trueb, 1986]. Only rarely, however, are characters of the cranial nerves and ganglia included in phylogenetic studies of fishes [e.g. Freihofer, 1978]. The fact that most characters of the cranial nerves are so conservative across all Craniata means that if a putative apomorphy is discovered, then it must be surveyed broadly to determine whether or not it is a synapomorphy at a very high level within Craniata (e.g. all Gnathostomata, all Osteichthyes, all Sarcopterygii, etc.). Unfortunately, our study cannot be a very complete test of the value of such neuroanatomical characters, because much essential comparative information is still missing. Despite the remarkable foundation provided by Allis [1889, 1897, 1920, 1922], Herrick [1899, 1900, 1901, 1944], Johnston [1905, 1908a, b], Norris [1924, 1925] and others, modern comparative work on the cranial nerves and ganglia is needed for most groups of fishes. This applies particularly to hagfishes and lampreys as well as to lungfishes, polypterids and most teleosts.

Table 1 summarizes the taxa and studies on which we base our phylogenetic comparisons. The studies referred to span more than a century and many changes in the terminology and interpretation of cranial nerves. Many phylogenetically interesting characters were treated only in passing by these authors, so we have confirmed their findings insofar as possible using serial sections of specimens in our own collections.

Table 2 lists the 38 characters developed from our study and a data matrix for the 12 taxa surveyed. The characters are numbered in anatomical order, and are introduced in our discussion in approximately this order. At this early stage in the phylogenetic study of cranial nerves we elected simply to score characters as present (1) or absent (0). Some characters listed in table 2 were difficult to score. For example, several characters concern ganglionic fusions, which we defined as intermixing of ganglionic cells within the same sheath. Several of the ganglionic fusions that we use as characters are known to develop relatively late in ontogeny, so in these cases, table 2 gives our best understanding of the adult condition. In the future, integrated comparative studies of the ganglia and rami of embryos, larval stages and adults should be made. As another general example of problematic characters, the patterns of the cranial nerves of hagfishes and lampreys are so different from those of gnathostomes that they pose special difficulties for scoring. We used our best estimate of the condition (scores followed by ? in tab. 2) in phylogenetic analyses.

Cladograms were generated and character distributions studied using PAUP 3.0 [Swofford, 1991] and MacClade 3.01 [Maddison and Maddison, 1992]. Taxa were rooted to a hypothetical ancestor in which all character states were 0.

Table 1. Summary of sources of comparative data on cranial nerves

	Eptatretus, Myxine	Petromyzon, Lampetra	Chimaera, Hydrolagus	Squalus, Mustelus	Polypterus	Acipenser	Lepisosteus	Amia	Neoceratodus	Protopterus, Lepidosiren	Latimeria	Ambystoma
Allis [1889, 1897]								X				
Allis [1920]						X	X	X				
Allis [1922]				X								
Boord and Campbell [1977]				X								
Coghill [1902]												X
Cole [1896]			X									
Cole and Dakin [1906]			X									
Damas [1951]		X										
El Toubi and Abdel-Aziz [1956]					X							
Fox [1965]									X			
Fritzsch [1987]											X	
Fritzsch et al. [1990]		X									X	
Gunther [1872]									X			
Hardisty [1982]	X	X										
Holmgren and van der Horst [1925]									X			
Johnston [1905, 1908a]		X										
Johnston [1908b]	X											
Landacre [1916]				X								
Lindström [1949]	X	X										
McCready and Boord [1976]				X								
Millot and Anthony [1958, 1965]											X	
Millot et al. [1978]											X	
Norris [1924]				X		X	X	X				
Norris [1925]						X	X	X				
Norris and Hughes [1920]				X								
Northcutt [1978]			X	X								
Northcutt [1992b]												X
Perhson [1949]									X		X	
Pinkus [1895]										X		
Sanders [1889]									X			
Smeets et al. [1983]			X	X								
Song and Northcutt [1991a, b]							X					
Worthington [1906]	X											

Accelerated transformation of characters (ACCTRAN) was used (most characters of the cranial nerves are likely to be very old, so that their absence in extant taxa will generally represent reversals). The cladogram shown in figure 20 is the single most parsimonious tree for the data from table 2, with a tree length of 56 steps, a consistency index of 0.68, and a retention index of 0.67. Listed on this cladogram are the apomorphic changes in character states. Unambiguous changes are those that occur in all possible cladistic reconstructions of the data (indicated by $\Rightarrow$ symbols); ambiguous changes (indicated by $\rightarrow$ symbols) are those required by this tree geometry but not by all possible trees. Our characters say nothing about branching order within some clades shown on figure 20 (e.g. the actinopterygians *Polypterus, Acipenser, Lepisosteus* and *Amia*), so in these cases, the figure reflects a consensus phylogeny based on characters summarized by Patterson [1982], Lauder and Liem [1983], Maisey [1986], and Grande and Bemis [1991].

Analysis of our data with MacClade shows that there are many nearly equally parsimonious trees which differ greatly in the position of *Latimeria*. Still, it is interesting that in our most parsimonious tree, *Latimeria* emerges as the sister taxon of *Ambystoma*. The phylogenetic position of coelacanths has been debated for many years (for examples, see Lagios [1979]; Compagno [1979]; Wiley [1979]; Rosen et al. [1981]; Forey [1987, 1991]; Schultze [1991]; and Cloutier [1991]). On the basis of our neuroanatomical characters and analysis, we regard coelacanths as osteichthyans and consider that they are probably the living sister group of tetrapods.

Olfactory Organ and Nerve

Our description of the olfactory organ and nerve is in complete agreement with that of Millot and Anthony [1965]. Several features of the olfactory system are relevant phylogenetically: the presence of an extensively folded olfactory epithelium restricted to the medial wall of the olfactory sac; the presence of pedunculated (i.e. non-sessile) olfactory bulbs; the absence of the terminal nerve, and the absence of a vomeronasal organ.

The olfactory sensory epithelium of *Latimeria* is restricted to the medial wall of the sac and is complexly fold-

Table 2. Character list and matrix

	Eptatretus, Myxine	Petromyzon, Lampetra	Chimaera, Hydrolagus	Squalus, Mustelus	Polypterus	Acipenser	Lepisosteus	Amia	Neocera-todus	Protopterus, Lepidosiren	Latimeria	Ambystoma
1 Folded olfactory epithelium	1	1	1	1	1	1	1	1	1	1	1	1
2 Short olfactory nerves	1	1	1	1	1	1	0	1	1	1	1	1
3 Pedunculated olfactory bulbs	0	0	0	1	0	0	0	0	1	0	1	0
4 Terminal nerve	0?	0?	0	1	1	1?	1	1?	1	1	0	1
5 Vomeronasal system	0	0	0	0	0	0	0	0	0	0	0	1
6 II elongate	0	0	0	0	0	0	0	0	0	0	1	0
7 Interdigitated decussation of II	1	1	1	1	1	1	1	1	1	1	1	1
8 Partial decussation of II	1	1	1	1	1	1	1	1	1	1	1	1
9 Ciliary ganglion	0	0	1	1	1	1?	1	1	1?	1	1	1
10 Ciliary ganglion located intracranially	0	0	0	0	0	0	0	0	0?	0?	1	0
11 III innervates superior rectus, inferior rectus, medial rectus and inferior oblique muscles	0	1	1	1	1	1	1	1	1	1	1	1
12 IV innervates superior oblique muscle	0	1	1	1	1	1	1	1	1	1	1	1
13 VI innervates lateral rectus muscle	0	1	1	1	1	1	1	1	1	1	1	1
14 VI innervates basicranial or ocular retractor muscle	0	0	0	0	0	0	0	0	0	0	1	1
15 Fusion of profundal and Vth ganglia	1	1	0	0	0	0	0	0	1	1	0	1
16 Profundal nerve innervates tubes of rostral organ	0	0	0	0	0	0	0	0	0	0	1	0
17 Maxillary and mandibular rami of V	0?	1	1	1	1	1	1	1	1	1	1	1
18 Buccal + maxillary complex	0	0	1	1	1	1	1	1	1	1	1	1
19 Superficial ophthalmic ramus of V	0	0	0	1	1	1	1	1	1	1	0	1
20 Pharyngeal, pre-, and post-trematic rami of VII	0	0	1	1	1	1	1	1	1	1	1	1
21 ADLLN	1	1	1	1	1	1	1	1	1	1	1	1
22 Superficial ophthalmic and buccal rami of ADLLN	0?	1	1	1	1	1	1	1	1	1	1	1
23 ADLLN innervates preopercular canal	0	0	0	0	0	0	0	0	0	0	1	0
24 ADLLN innervates rostral sac of rostral organ	0	0	0	0	0	0	0	0	0	0	1	0
25 AVLLN	0	1	1	1	1	1	1	1	1	1	1	1
26 g AV+VII	0	0	0	0	0	0	0	0	1	1	1	1
27 OLLN	0	1?	1	1	1	1	1	1	1	1	1	0
28 Spiracular ramus of OLLN	0	0?	1	1	0	1	1	1	1	1	1	0
29 Otic commissure	0	0?	0	0	0	0	0	0	0	0	1	0
30 MLLN	0	1?	0	1	1	1	1	1	1	1	1	1
31 STLLN	1?	1?	1	1	1	1	1	1	1	1	1	1
32 PLLN	0	1	1	1	1	1	1	1	1	1	1	1
33 Dorsal ramus of PLLN	0	1?	1	1	1	1	1	1	1	1	1	1
34 Ventral ramus of PLLN	0	1?	0?	1	0	0	0	0	1	1	0	1
35 Medial and lateral ganglia of IX	0	0	0	0	0	0	0	0	0?	0	1	1
36 Pharyngeal, pre-. and post-trematic rami of IX	0	0?	1	1	1	1	1	1	1	1	1	1
37 Medial and lateral ganglia of X	0	0	0	0	1	1	1	1	1	1	1	0
38 Pharyngeal, pre-, and post-trematic rami of $X_{1,2,3}$	0	0?	1	1	1	1	1	1	1	1	1	1

Character states are based on data from the present study and literature summarized in table 1.
Characters are scored 0 (absent) or 1 (present). Scores followed by a ? indicate uncertainty about the condition in that taxon.

ed into three dorsal and two ventral lobes. A folded olfactory epithelium is found in all lineages of craniates (character 1; tab.2, fig.20), however, its location within the olfactory sac and the degree of folding varies among those craniates that have been studied. In *Polypterus*, for example, the five lobes of the olfactory epithelium are arrayed in a rosette completely around the circumference of the olfac-

tory sac [Kleerekoper, 1969: fig.24]. In *Protopterus* [Derivot, 1984: fig.2], the folds of the sensory epithelium are restricted to the dorsomedial and ventromedial walls of the olfactory sac. The location and degree of folding may prove phylogenetically important, but survey is still required.

In *Latimeria*, the fascicles of the olfactory nerve are extremely short, and they terminate in the olfactory bulb

Discussion

which is located immediately caudal to the olfactory sac. The secondary olfactory tracts arising from cells in the olfactory bulb, however, form a greatly elongated olfactory peduncle prior to terminating in the telencephalic hemispheres. In all anamniotes except gars and certain teleosts, the olfactory nerves are short, so the condition of the olfactory nerves in *Latimeria* represents the ancestral condition for craniates (character 2; tab.2, fig.20). Elongated olfactory peduncles are found in most elasmobranchs, *Latimeria*, *Neoceratodus*, and some teleosts, whereas sessile olfactory bulbs (i.e. non-pedunculated) occur in all other anamniotes [Northcutt, 1987]. In our analysis, the presence of pedunculated olfactory tracts evolved convergently in *Squalus*, *Neoceratodus*, and *Latimeria* (character 3; tab.2, fig.20).

Like Millot and Anthony [1965], we were unable to find a terminal nerve in *Latimeria*. Immunohistochemical studies of the forebrain are most likely to reveal a terminal nerve in *Latimeria* if one exists. The terminal nerve may exist in lampreys [von Bartheld et al., 1987; Northcutt and Puzdrowski, 1988], but probably does not; the condition in hagfishes remains unknown. Except for chimaeroids, the terminal nerve has been reported in all lineages of gnathostomes that have been studied and it was interpreted by Northcutt [1985, p. 103] to be a derived character of gnathostomes. In our cladogram, the terminal nerve appears at the level of gnathostomes and is lost independently in *Chimaera* and *Latimeria* (character 4; tab.2, fig.20).

In tetrapods, an accessory olfactory organ (vomeronasal or Jacobson's organ) arises as a ventral diverticulum in the floor of the olfactory sac. This diverticulum may remain in continuity with the sac (as in amphibians and *Sphenodon*) or it may be a separate organ (as in amniotes generally). The axons of the receptor cells of the vomeronasal organ form a distinct bundle, termed the vomeronasal nerve, which terminates in a distinct portion of the olfactory bulb, termed the accessory olfactory bulb [see Northcutt, 1987 for review]. Several workers have claimed that a vomeronasal organ is present in lungfishes [e.g., Rudebeck, 1944, 1945; Schnitzlein and Crosby, 1967; Rosen et al., 1981], whereas others have rejected these claims [Bertmar, 1965; Derivot, 1984; Northcutt, 1987], and this is the condition scored in table 2. *Latimeria* offers no evidence of a vomeronasal system, so it appears likely that it is a synapomorphy of tetrapods (character 5; tab.2, fig.20).

Optic Nerve

There are four points regarding the course and organization of the optic nerve. First is the topographical origin of the optic nerve from the eye. We find that the optic nerve originates from the dorsal hemi-retina of the eye, whereas Millot and Anthony [1965, p. 42] state that it arises from the ventral hemi-retina. We do not have a ready explanation for this difference, although it may be due to ontogenetic or individual variation; this feature has not been surveyed adequately to include it in table 2. The short length and general course of the optic nerve in the pup resemble the condition in most other anamniotes, although the nerve is greatly elongated in adult *Latimeria*, as clearly documented by Millot and Anthony [1965, their fig.3, 16]. Many cranial features of *Latimeria* show marked allometric elongation during postnatal growth [see Anthony, 1980, fig.8], and it is clear that the autapomorphic elongation of the optic nerve of adult *Latimeria* is also such a feature (character 6; tab.2, fig.20).

As noted by Millot and Anthony [1965], the optic nerve of *Latimeria* is deeply plicated (pleated as used by Northcutt and Wullimann [1988] is a synonym). A plicated nerve does not occur in hagfishes or lampreys but is found in many actinopterygians surveyed by Northcutt and Wullimann [1988, pp. 520–521]. There appears to be much variation in the presence of plication. For example, *Polypterus palmas* has a plicated nerve, whereas *Erpetoichthys calabaricus* does not; similarly, *Polyodon spathula* exhibits plication, but *Scaphirhynchus platorynchus* does not. Northcutt and Wullimann [1988: p. 519] interpreted that a plicated optic nerve might be a synapomorphy of actinopterygians; however, its presence in *Latimeria* calls that interpretation into question. Additional phylogenetic survey and better definition of this feature is needed.

In *Latimeria* the fascicles of the right and left optic nerves interdigitate to form the optic chiasm. Among craniates, there are two patterns of decussation of fibers of the optic nerve. A chiasm formed by interdigitation of the fascicles (as in *Latimeria*) occurs in all craniates except teleosts (the distribution has not been fully surveyed, but this may be a synapomorphy of Teleostei; see Northcutt and Wullimann [1988]. The nerves do not interdigitate in teleosts but instead simply cross over each other, with each nerve retaining its integrity, or in some cases one nerve penetrates the other. Both of these patterns reported for teleosts must be regarded as derived. Clearly, the interdigitated decussation of the optic nerves seen in *Latimeria* must be the plesiomorphic condition for craniates (character 7; tab.2, fig.20).

A related issue is whether the decussation is complete or partial. In complete decussation, all optic nerve fibers project to nuclei in the contralateral side of the brain, whereas in partial decussation, some fibers of each optic nerve pro-

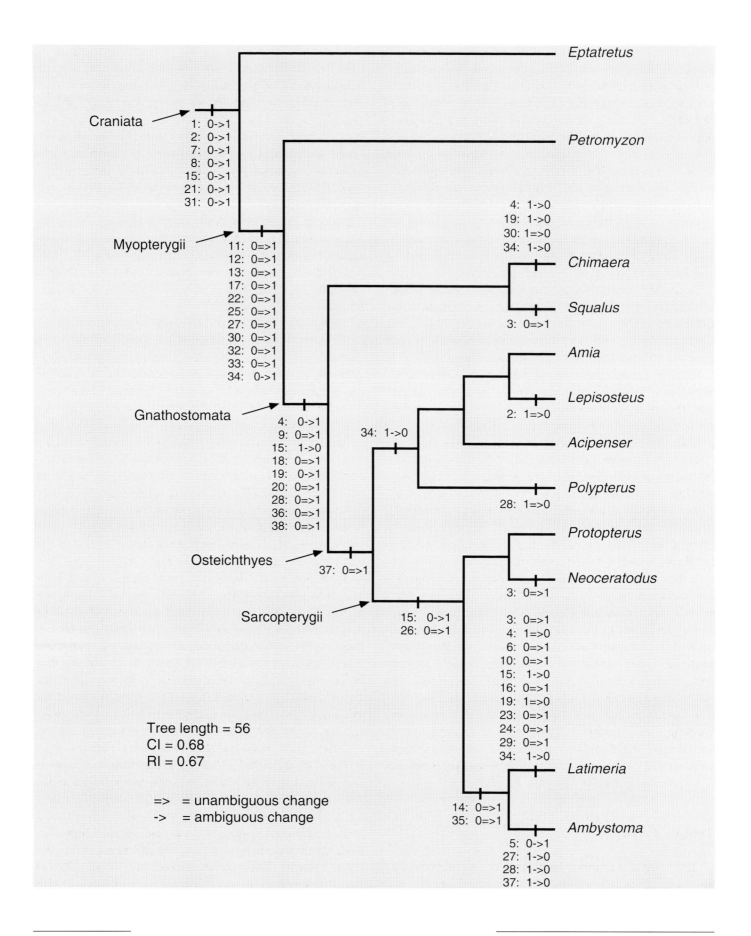

Craniata
1: 0->1
2: 0->1
7: 0->1
8: 0->1
15: 0->1
21: 0->1
31: 0->1

Myopterygii
11: 0=>1
12: 0=>1
13: 0=>1
17: 0=>1
22: 0=>1
25: 0=>1
27: 0=>1
30: 0=>1
32: 0=>1
33: 0=>1
34: 0->1

Gnathostomata
4: 0->1
9: 0=>1
15: 1->0
18: 0=>1
19: 0->1
20: 0=>1
28: 0=>1
36: 0=>1
38: 0=>1

Osteichthyes
37: 0=>1

Sarcopterygii
15: 0->1
26: 0=>1

Tree length = 56
CI = 0.68
RI = 0.67

=> = unambiguous change
-> = ambiguous change

Eptatretus

Petromyzon

4: 1->0
19: 1->0
30: 1=>0
34: 1->0

Chimaera

Squalus
3: 0=>1

34: 1->0

Amia

Lepisosteus
2: 1=>0

Acipenser

Polypterus
28: 1=>0

Protopterus

Neoceratodus
3: 0=>1

3: 0=>1
4: 1->0
6: 0=>1
10: 0=>1
15: 1->0
16: 0=>1
19: 1=>0
23: 0=>1
24: 0=>1
29: 0=>1
34: 1->0

Latimeria

14: 0=>1
35: 0=>1

Ambystoma
5: 0->1
27: 1->0
28: 1->0
37: 1->0

ject to ipsilateral nuclei. Millot and Anthony [1965, p. 44] concluded that *Latimeria* has only partial optic decussation and that it differs from other fishes in this respect. Numerous recent studies, however [summarized in Butler and Northcutt, 1992], indicate that total decussation only occurs in some teleosts and that partial decussation is the primitive condition for craniates (character 8; tab.2, fig.20). Even though we lack experimental confirmation, it is probable that *Latimeria* exhibits partial decussation and therefore retains the primitive condition for craniates.

Nerves of the Extraocular Muscles

We are in general agreement with Millot and Anthony [1965] regarding the major subdivisions of the oculomotor and trochlear nerves and the muscles they innervate, although our interpretation of the nerves to the extraocular muscles differs from theirs in two major aspects. First, we find that *Latimeria* has a ciliary ganglion implying that it has visceral motor innervation of the eye. Second, we find that the basicranial muscle is innervated by the abducent nerve in contrast to their interpretation that this muscle is innervated by a branch of the vagal nerve.

In gnathostomes generally there is a ciliary ganglion (character 9; tab.2, fig.20). It is composed of the cell bodies of the second-order visceral motoneurons of the parasympathetic system, and typically lies between the ramus of the profundal nerve and the trunk of the oculomotor nerve [Allis, 1897; Norris and Hughes, 1920; Norris, 1925; Jarvik 1980]. The condition in *Amia* (fig.21A) serves as a general case. The preganglionic fibers to the ciliary ganglion are the axons of the Edinger-Westphal nucleus, which is located in the midbrain tegmentum (ViM(EW); fig.21). These preganglionic fibers reach the ganglion by initially traveling through the trunk of the oculomotor nerve and subsequently forming a short root of the ciliary ganglion (short; fig.21) interconnecting the oculomotor nerve with the ciliary ganglion. The axons of the cells of the ciliary ganglion (i.e. its postganglionic fibers) pass into the eye, forming a short ciliary ramus (scr; fig.21A), which innervates the intrinsic muscles and glandular tissue of the eye. In addition to the ciliary ganglion's connection with the trunk

Fig. 20. Cladogram of 12 taxa of living craniates based on data in table 2. This is the most parsimonious cladogram based on these data, but there are many other nearly equally parsimonious trees. All apomorphic changes in characters are indicated. Changes indicated as unambiguous occur in all cladograms based on the data from table 2; ambiguous changes occur only in a subset of all possible cladograms based on these data.

of the oculomotor nerve, it also is interconnected with the trunk of the profundal nerve. Sensory neurons of the profundal nerve innervate the eye by two routes. In the first, more circuitous route, the peripheral processes pass to the ciliary ganglion via the long root of the ciliary ganglion (long; fig.21A), from which they travel with the postganglionic fibers of the ciliary ganglion in the short ciliary ramus to reach the eye. In the second route, the processes of the visceral sensory neurons innervate the eye directly via the long ciliary ramus (1cr; fig.21).

Millot and Anthony [1965, p. 80] failed to find a ciliary ganglion in *Latimeria* or any branch of the oculomotor nerve innervating the eye. However, they did note two rami arising from the profundal nerve and innervating the eye, which they termed ciliary 'nerves' [Millot and Anthony, 1965; their fig.19 on which their labels for the abducent nerve 'n. VI' and the ciliary nerve 'n. cil.' are obviously reversed]. Because they did not find the ciliary ganglion, or identify a ramus of the oculomotor nerve innervating the eye, they concluded that there was no parasympathetic innervation of the eye in *Latimeria* and that their two ciliary nerves arising from the profundal nerve carry only visceral sensory information from the eye. In this context, they also noted the complete lack of intrinsic muscles in the eye of *Latimeria*, and suggested that this is correlated with a deep-sea habitat.

In tracing the oculomotor nerve, we discovered a ganglion embedded in the nerve which we can only interpret as the ciliary ganglion. In this regard, *Latimeria* exhibits what we consider to be a synapomorphy of gnathostomes (character 9; tab.2, fig.20). The condition in *Latimeria* is unusual, however, in that the ganglion is located intracranially rather than in the orbit. This does not occur in any other craniates we surveyed, so we interpret this location as an autapomorphy of *Latimeria* (character 10; tab.2, fig.20). Unlike Millot and Anthony [1965], we were able to trace a ventral ramule of the dorsal ramus of the oculomotor nerve toward the eye, where it is joined by the second ramule to arise from the profundal nerve (p2, fig.2A, 21B). Distal to this anastomosis, the combined fibers of the oculomotor and profundal nerves form dorsal and ventral ciliary 'nerves', as described by Millot and Anthony [1965]. We thus interpret these relationships very differently from Millot and Anthony [1965]. Given the presence of ganglion cells embedded in the root of the oculomotor nerve, and a connection between the oculomotor nerve and the profundal nerve ramule that innervates the eye, we conclude that visceral motor fibers to the eye must exist. Assuming that Millot and Anthony [1965] correctly interpreted the absence of intrinsic ocular muscles in *Latimeria*, then the

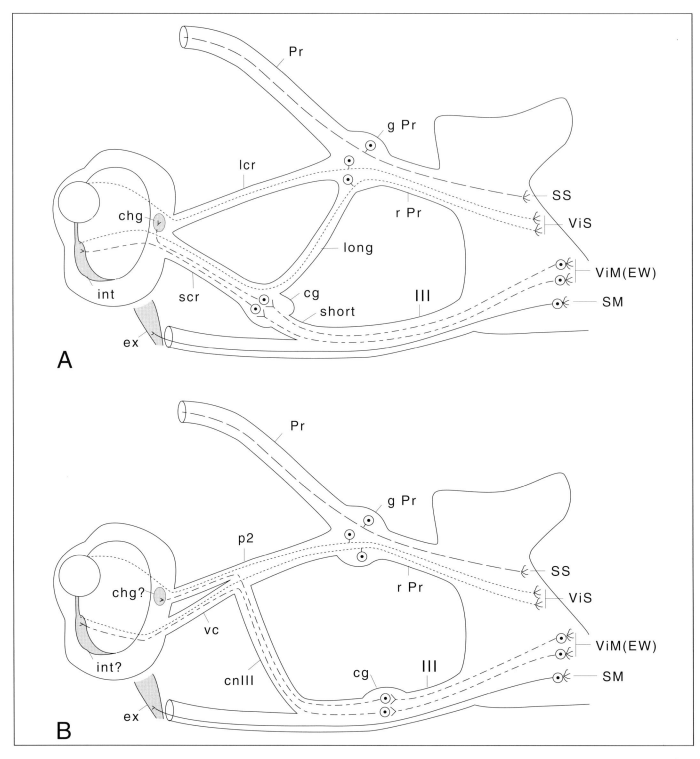

Fig. 21. Diagram of the ciliary 'nerves' of *Amia* and *Latimeria*. **A** Ciliary 'nerves' of *Amia* redrawn from Jarvik [1980, vol. 2, fig. 19]. **B** Our interpretation of the ciliary 'nerves' of *Latimeria*. See text for explanation.

parasympathetic fibers from the ciliary ganglion presumably innervate glandular tissue or blood vessels of the eye (intrinsic musculature and glandular tissue indicated by int? and chg? in fig. 21B). Given the anastomosis of the ventral ramule of the dorsal ramus of the oculomotor nerve with the second ramule of the profundal nerve prior to its division into dorsal and ventral ciliary nerves, we cannot state if both the dorsal and ventral ciliary nerves carry the postganglionic fibers from the ciliary ganglion. Furthermore, because of the proximal position of the ciliary ganglion in the oculomotor nerve, it is impossible to recognize distinct short or long roots of the ciliary ganglion in *Latimeria*. The two ciliary nerves that we recognize in *Latimeria* must contain the same complement of fibers as the short and long ciliary rami of other gnathostomes, but we cannot homologize them. Although each of these morphological features (e.g. absence of short root of ciliary ganglion, absence of long ciliary ramus, etc.) may appear to be a discrete phylogenetic character, in fact they all derive from the proximal location of the ciliary ganglion within the trunk of the oculomotor nerve, and therefore they should not be considered separate autapomorphies. A final related point concerns the phylogenetic distribution of the anastomosis of the oculomotor and profundal nerves. Although Allis [1922] did not observe this, El-Toubi and Abdel-Aziz [1956] did. The condition of the ciliary 'nerves' and ganglion in *Polypterus* should be rechecked.

As in all craniates (except hagfishes, in which there has been secondary reduction of the eyes; see Wicht and Northcutt [1990]), the oculomotor nerve of *Latimeria* innervates the inferior oblique, superior rectus, inferior rectus, and medial rectus muscles (character 11; tab. 2, fig. 20) and the trochlear nerve innervates the superior oblique muscle (character 12; tab. 2, fig. 20). Thus there is nothing unusual about the somatic motor components of these nerves in *Latimeria*.

The abducent nerve in *Latimeria* not only innervates the lateral rectus muscle (character 13; tab. 2, fig. 20) but also the basicranial muscle (character 14; tab. 2, fig. 20). Millot and Anthony [1965, p. 55] noted great difficulty in tracing the abducent nerve in dissection. From its roots arising in the floor of the medulla at the level of the glossopharyngeal nerve, they were able to follow its course through the cartilages of the otic region, rostrally along the dorsal surface of the basicranial muscle, then dorsally into the orbit to the lateral rectus muscle. In spite of the abducent nerve's close association with the basicranial muscle, Millot and Anthony [1965] concluded that this muscle was innervated by a branch of the vagal nerve ['n. sousc.', Millot and Anthony, 1965, fig. 31]. In contrast, we have shown that the abducent nerve gives off several branches that innervate the basicranial muscle from its dorsal surface [Bemis and Northcutt, 1991]. These branches include a prominent recurrent ramus which passes nearly to the caudal pole of the muscle, as well as two large, centrally located intramuscular rami (r VI, m VI; fig. 3). We interpret Millot and Anthony's [1965] 'n. sousc.' as the first pharyngeal ramus of the vagal nerve (its medial ramule, m1p X, is indicated in our fig. 2B) and find no evidence of any vagal innervation of the basicranial muscle. Thus it is no longer necessary to postulate a 'nervus rarus' as the motor nerve of the basicranial muscle, as proposed by Bjerring [1972].

The homologies of the basicranial muscle and its innervation by the abducent nerve remain uncertain, although we have proposed [Bemis and Northcutt, 1991] that the muscle in *Latimeria* is homologous to the eye and tentacle retractor muscles (*m. retractor bulbi* and *m. retractor tentaculi*, respectively) of amphibians and possibly to the caudal rectus muscle of lampreys [Fritzsch et al., 1990]. Embryological data showing that all of these muscles arise from the same portion of the paraxial mesoderm of the head might confirm our interpretation, but early embryological material for *Latimeria* is still unknown and many details of head development in lampreys only now are being studied [Langille and Hall, 1988]. We also note that there may be much to learn about preotic segmentation in gnathostomes [Bemis and Grande, 1992]. For instance, Bjerring [1977] interpreted that larval *Amia* develop a basicranial muscle in the wall of the orbit, although he did not suggest that it is innervated by the abducent nerve. Further study of the phylogenetic distribution of muscles innervated by the abducent nerve is needed, but we tentatively accept this as a synapomorphy of coelacanths and tetrapods (character 14; tab. 2, fig. 20).

Profundal Nerve

Although Millot and Anthony [1965, p. 47] regarded the profundal nerve as a division of the trigeminal nerve, they noted that the peripheral course of the profundal nerve is totally separate from that of the trigeminal nerve. We confirm this basic observation about the separate peripheral distribution of profundal and trigeminal fibers, and we note that the sensory ganglion and roots of the profundal nerve also are separate from the sensory ganglion and roots of the trigeminal nerve. Thus the profundal nerve should be considered a phylogenetically independent cranial nerve rather than a division of the trigeminal nerve (character 15; tab. 2, fig. 20). Millot and Anthony's assertion [1965, p. 83] that separate profundal and trigeminal nerves are unique to *Latimeria* is incorrect. The profundal nerve develops from a placode, whereas the trigeminal nerve develops from neural crest [Stone, 1922]. Fused profundal and trigeminal ganglia occur in hagfishes [Marinelli and Strenger, 1954] and lampreys [Johnston, 1905]. In chimaeras [Cole, 1896], elasmobranchs [Norris and Hughes, 1920; McCready and Boord, 1976] and basal actinopterygians [Norris, 1925; Song and Northcutt, 1991a], however, the profundal and trigeminal ganglia are separate. Adult *Polypterus* reportedly have a common root for the profundal and trigeminal nerves [El Toubi and Abdel-Aziz, 1956], although the ganglia remain separate. In some teleosts, profundal and trigeminal ganglia are fused. Fusion of the profundal and trigeminal ganglia also occurs in lungfishes and tetrapods, but it is far from clear that these fusions should be considered homologous. In *Lepidosiren* and *Neoceratodus* there is a single preotic ganglionic complex [Fox, 1965]. This presumably results by fusion of the profundal, trigeminal, facial, anterodorsal lateral line, anteroventral lateral line, and otic lateral line ganglia, but this interpretation should be confirmed by embryological studies. In embryonic amphibians and amniotes, the profundal and trigeminal nerves are initially separate but fuse later in ontogeny [Coghill, 1916; Stone, 1922]. The condition of separate profundal and trigeminal ganglia in *Latimeria* is a retention of a synapomorphy at the level of gnathostomes.

A final point is that it is misleading to refer to a 'Gasserian ganglion' in those craniates with separate profundal and trigeminal ganglia. The term 'Gasserian ganglion' can correctly be applied to the condition in those tetrapods in which fusion is complete, but it is clear that this term cannot be applied to either of the separate ganglia as found in *Latimeria* (for a view on this problem, see Jollie [1962, p. 394]).

The profundal nerve in *Latimeria* appears to be a purely somatosensory nerve which innervates the skin of the snout and the mucus membranes lining the rostral tubes. We disagree with Millot and Anthony's interpretation [1965, fig. 21] that ramules of the profundal nerve anastomose with the superficial ophthalmic ramus of the anterodorsal lateral line nerve. Rather, we find that those ramules of the profundal nerve that travel adjacent to the superficial ophthalmic ramus pass medial to it without exchanging fibers before exiting through foramina to innervate the overlying skin.

The innervation of a portion of the rostral organ by ramules 4 to 8 of the profundal nerve warrants special comment (character 16; tab. 2, fig. 20). We consider the rostral organ homologous to clusters of ampullae of Lorenzini [Bemis and Hetherington, 1982; also see section on antero-

dorsal lateral line nerve, below]. The rostral organ is unknown in other craniates and is probably a synapomorphy of coelacanths [Cloutier, 1991, p. 40]. It consists of three pairs of rostral tubes (posterior superior rostral tube, posterior inferior rostral tube and anterior rostral tube) which lead medially to a spongy tissue termed the rostral sac. In turn, the rostral sac is subdivided into portions associated with each of the rostral tubes [Millot and Anthony, 1965]. Ramules of the profundal ramus innervate the mucosa of the rostral tubes but not the putative electroreceptors of the rostral sac. The account by Millot and Anthony [1965, fig. 21] is incorrect in several respects. First, no substantial trigeminal component travels with the superficial ophthalmic ramus of the anterodorsal lateral line nerve in the snout, so the innervation of the posterior superior and posterior inferior portions of the rostral sac must be entirely from the anterodorsal lateral line nerve. Second, because Millot and Anthony [1965] did not realize that the buccal ramus of the anterodorsal lateral line nerve fuses with the maxillary ramus of the trigeminal to form the buccal + maxillary complex, they misinterpreted the innervation of the anterior rostral sac as coming from the maxillary branch of the trigeminal nerve. We find that the epithelium of the anterior rostral sac is innervated by fibers from the buccal ramus of the anterodorsal lateral line nerve. Thus, all three portions of the rostral sac are innervated by the anterodorsal lateral line nerve, although the fibers reach the rostral sac by traveling in two different rami. Third, Millot and Anthony [1965] did not detect the innervation of the mucosa of the rostral tubes by the profundal nerve, whereas our observations clearly indicate this. The rostral organ is thus innervated by two separate cranial nerves: the superficial ophthalmic and buccal rami of the anterodorsal lateral line nerve innervate all of the putative electroreceptors of the rostral sac, whereas the profundal nerve innervates the mucus membranes of the rostral tubes, presumably to carry pain and temperature information from that epithelium. We have not found any reports about innervation of the membranous walls of the ampullae of Lorenzini in chondrichthyans, but, based on the condition of the rostral tubes in *Latimeria*, this ought to be examined.

Trigeminal Nerve

Our description of the peripheral distribution of the maxillary and mandibular rami of the trigeminal nerve closely agrees with that of Millot and Anthony [1965, their fig. 20]. There are many problems with their account, however. Chiefly, their concept of the organization of the trigeminal, facial and preotic lateral line nerves was affected by their lack of histological material and inability to recognize cranial ganglia and their associated roots and trunks. To understand the organization of the trigeminal nerve, it is first necessary to review all of these preotic ganglia and their rami (fig. 22). Our histological material reveals five distinct ganglia in the preotic region ventral to the auricular lobe of the cerebellum (g Pr, g V, G AD, g O, g AV + VII; fig. 2). The sensory ganglion of the profundal nerve is the most medial of these five ganglia, and its sensory root is the most rostral to enter the medulla (g Pr; fig. 2A). The sensory ganglion of the trigeminal nerve lies immediately lateral to the profundal ganglion and nerve, and its sensory and motor roots enter the medulla caudal to the sensory root of the profundal nerve (g V; fig. 2A). The trigeminal trunk (t V; fig. 2B) arises from the rostral pole of the trigeminal sensory ganglion (this trunk corresponds to the trigeminal nerve, 'n. V', of Millot and Anthony [1965, fig. 17], redrawn in our figure 22A. On exiting the cranium, the trigeminal trunk divides into maxillary and mandibular rami (max, m V; fig. 2B, 22B). Our material indicates that a distinct superficial ophthalmic ramus of the trigeminal nerve does not exist in *Latimeria*, although small ramules do arise from the rostral pole of the trigeminal ganglion and the proximal portion of the trigeminal trunk. These ramules pass dorsally through the cranium to innervate the overlying skin in the region of levels RC 500 to RC 700. We consider these ramules homologous to the superficial ophthalmic ramus of the trigeminal reported in other anamniotes (discussed in detail in the section on anterodorsal lateral line nerve, below).

A third sensory ganglion lies dorsal to the caudal half of the trigeminal ganglion. This ganglion and its rami we identify as the anterodorsal lateral line nerve (g AD; fig. 2A). Distal to the anterodorsal ganglion, and dorsal to the trigeminal trunk, the short trunk of the anterodorsal lateral line nerve divides into a dorsal ramus (superficial ophthalmic ramus of the anterodorsal lateral line nerve) and a ventral ramus (buccal ramus of the anterodorsal lateral line nerve). The superficial ophthalmic ramus of the anterodorsal lateral line nerve continues within the neurocranium dorsally and laterally, enters its canal, and emerges in the orbit. The buccal ramus of the anterodorsal lateral line nerve passes ventromedially to anastomose with the maxillary ramus of the trigeminal trunk. These observations differ from the statements and figures of Millot and Anthony [1965]. They interpreted the ganglion and trunk of the anterodorsal lateral line nerve as the proximal portion of the 'superficial ophthalmic nerve' (fig. 22A, 'n. ophth.

sup.'), although they correctly figured the division of the trunk of our anterodorsal lateral line nerve into superficial ophthalmic and buccal rami, and the fusion of the buccal ramus with the maxillary ramus of the trigeminal nerve (fig. 22A).

A fourth sensory ganglion, which we interpret as the ganglion of the otic lateral line nerve, lies adjacent and ventrolateral to the ganglion of the anterodorsal lateral line nerve (g O; fig. 2A). The dorsally directed root of the otic ganglion fuses with the ventral root of the anterodorsal lateral line nerve; distally the otic ganglion gives rise to anterior and posterior otic rami. Some fibers from the trigeminal ganglion pass dorsally through the anterodorsal lateral line ganglion to enter the anterior ramus of the otic lateral line nerve. This exchange of sensory fibers appears to correspond to an anastomosis indicated by Millot and Anthony [1965], and shown in our figure 22A as 'an. V–VII'.

A fifth preotic sensory ganglion occurs ventral and caudal to the other four ganglia. We interpret this as a fusion of the ganglia of the anteroventral lateral line and facial nerves, based on the occurrence of two distinct cell populations within this single ganglionic complex. The most dorsal cells of the ganglion complex, for example, are large with palely staining cytoplasm (fig. 14B), and appear identical to the ganglionic cells of the other lateral line nerves. The phylogenetic distribution of this character is very interesting (character 26; tab. 2, fig. 20). A comparable fused ganglion of the anteroventral lateral line and facial nerves occurs in salamanders [Northcutt, 1992b], where it is known to develop by the fusion of separate placodal (for the anteroventral ganglion) and neural crest (for the facial ganglion) precursors late in ontogeny [Coghill, 1916]. This may be a synapomorphy of *Latimeria* and tetrapods. The condition in lungfishes complicates matters, however, because all preotic ganglia are fused into a single ganglionic complex (e.g., trigeminal, lateral line and profundal ganglia are all fused). If we regard g AV + VII as a sarcopterygian character, and the additional fusions of all preotic ganglia as a synapomorphy of lungfishes, then the presence of g AV + VII says nothing about relationships among lungfishes, coelacanths and tetrapods. On the whole, this is the more conservative view, and is the one reflected in our analysis (character 26; tab. 2, fig. 20).

There is another discrepancy between our interpretation of the preotic nerves and that of Millot and Anthony [1965], as illustrated by figure 22. In their ventral view of the brain and nerves (fig. 22A), two structures are labeled as portions of the anterior lateral line nerve: 'a.r.n. lat. a.' and 'p.r.n. lat. a.'. The posterior structure ('p.r.n. lat. a.'), which passes laterally to join the facial nerve, corresponds to our anteroventral lateral line nerve supplying the mandibular canal (m AV; fig. 22B), but their anterior structure ('a.r.n. lat. a.') does not appear to have a correspondent in the pup. This area lies in the rostral portion of the 'gap' in our sections, so, if the bundle occupied fewer than ten sections, it is conceivable that we failed to recognize it for this reason. Millot and Anthony interpreted the 'a.r.n. lat. a.' as passing rostrally to divide into dorsal and ventral ramules; their dorsal ramule ('d.r.a.r.n. lat. a.') is shown fusing with their superficial ophthalmic nerve, and their ventral branch ('v.r.a.r.n. lat. a.') is shown fusing with their trigeminal trunk. We can recognize part of this pattern in the pup, because the trunk of our anterodorsal lateral line nerve gives off the large buccal ramus, which joins the maxillary ramus of the trigeminal and could correspond to Millot and Anthony's ventral ramule 'v.r.a.r.n. lat. a.'. We cannot, however, agree with their interpretation that a dorsal branch contributes to the superficial ophthalmic ramus. For reasons that will be outlined in the section on lateral line nerves, we suggest that their anterior root ('a.r.n. lat. a.'), if it exists, is probably a component of the anteroventral lateral line nerve that joins the buccal ramus of the anterodorsal lateral line nerve in order to innervate the neuromasts of the preopercular line. If Millot and Anthony's diagram correctly represents the condition in adult *Latimeria*, then this component of the anteroventral lateral line nerve may appear as a discrete bundle in the adult, perhaps due to ontogenetic elongation of the snout.

In *Latimeria* the trigeminal nerve has distinct maxillary and mandibular rami, as it does in myopterygians (character 17; tab. 2, fig. 20). In *Latimeria* as in all other gnathostomes, the maxillary ramus of the trigeminal is joined by the buccal ramus of the anterodorsal lateral line nerve to form a fused buccal + maxillary complex, which carries both lateral line and somatosensory components (character 18; tab. 2, fig. 20). The buccal component of the buccal + maxillary complex innervates the neuromasts of the infraorbital canal, as well as the putative electroreceptors of the anterior rostral sac. The maxillary component of the buccal + maxillary complex innervates the skin below the eye and the skin of the ventrolateral surface of the snout. The mandibular ramus carries sensory fibers that innervate the skin of the lower jaw as well as motor fibers for the mandibular arch muscles. Although a maxillary ramus of the trigeminal nerve is present in adult *Petromyzon* [Johnston, 1905], it does not fuse with the buccalis ramus. It thus appears that character 18 is a synapomorphy of gnathostomes.

The trigeminal nerve of *Latimeria* lacks a distinct superficial ophthalmic ramus and thus *Latimeria* has secondarily lost the superficial ophthalmic complex (character 19; tab. 2, fig. 20). In *Petromyzon*, Johnston [1905] reported that the superficial ophthalmic ramus of the anterodorsal lateral line nerve fused with the profundal nerve; this should be reconfirmed. In *Chimaera*, the superficial ophthalmic ramus of the trigeminal nerve lies adjacent to but does not fuse with the anterodorsal lateral line nerve [Cole, 1896, p. 646]. In other anamniotes [*Ambystoma*, Coghill, 1902; *Squalus*, Norris and Hughes, 1920; *Amia*, *Lepisosteus*, *Acipenser*, Norris, 1925] the superficial ophthalmic complex is believed to receive equal contributions from the trigeminal nerve and the anterodorsal lateral line nerve (termed the facial lateral line component in older literature). The trigeminal component of the complex in these taxa is believed to carry pain and temperature fibers from the skin of the snout. In *Latimeria*, however, most of the skin between the eyes and on the dorsal surface of the snout is innervated by the profundal nerve. The only trigeminal fibers associated with the skin of the dorsal side of the head innervate the area immediately posterior to the eye. These fibers travel in ramules that issue from the proximal portion of the trigeminal trunk, and we believe they are the only components of the trigeminal nerve that could be homologous to the superficial ophthalmic ramus of the trigeminal nerve in classical interpretations. If the classical concept of the superficial ophthalmic complex in other anamniotic gnathostomes is correct, then the condition in *Latimeria* is an autapomorphy. Application of horseradish peroxidase to the superficial ophthalmic complex in *Ambystoma*, however, labeled only a few cells in the trigeminal ganglion [Northcutt, 1992b], thus indicating that most fibers of the superficial ophthalmic complex in amphibians are anterodorsal lateral line fibers rather than trigeminal fibers. We need more comparative experimental studies of other anamniotes, focusing on the extent of trigeminal contributions to the superficial ophthalmic complex, before we can conclude with certainty that the condition in *Latimeria* is unique.

Facial Nerve

There are several discrepancies between Millot and Anthony's [1965] account and our observations of the facial nerve and its rami. With one exception, the discrepancies we discuss result from their failure to recognize the positions and relationships of the preotic sensory ganglia.

Millot and Anthony [1965] described an otic ramus arising from the trunk of the facial nerve prior to its penetration of the cranial wall. We discovered that their otic ramus actually arises from a distinct ganglion located ventral to the ganglion of the anterodorsal lateral line nerve (g O; fig.2A), and, therefore, it should be regarded as an independent otic lateral line nerve as found in myopterygians generally (character 27; tab.2, fig.20). While we agree with Millot and Anthony [1965, p. 58] that the trunk of this otic lateral line nerve divides into anterior and posterior rami, we differ regarding the peripheral course of these rami and the organs they innervate. Millot and Anthony [1965] claim that the anterior ramus of the otic lateral line nerve innervates three neuromasts of the otic sensory canal, whereas we have been able to trace this ramus only to the most rostral neuromast of the otic sensory canal (otc; fig.1B). All remaining neuromasts of the otic sensory canal are innervated by the posterior ramus of the otic lateral line nerve. In addition, as the posterior ramus of the otic lateral line nerve approaches the neurocranial wall, it issues a ramule, which passes over the dorsal surface of the facial nerve, then ventrally towards the medial wall of the spiracular chamber. This spiracular ramule was missed by Millot and Anthony [1965]; it is almost certainly a synapomorphy at the level of gnathostomes (character 28; tab.2, fig.20). We agree with Millot and Anthony [1965] that the posterior ramus of the otic lateral line nerve turns caudally to anastomose with postotic lateral line nerves, but we note that the anastomosis actually occurs with the middle lateral line nerve and the ventral ramus of the supratemporal lateral line nerve. Because Millot and Anthony [1965, fig.36] did not recognize middle and supratemporal lateral line nerves they merely reported that the caudally directed ramus of the otic lateral line nerve anastomoses with the anterior branch of the posterior lateral line nerve. They termed the caudal portion of the posterior ramus of the otic lateral line nerve the 'recurrent ramus of the facial nerve' ['r. rec. VII', Millot and Anthony, 1965, fig.36]; we have termed it the otic commissure (oc; fig.2A). This is an unusual anastomosis, apparently present only in *Latimeria* (the condition in adult *Petromyzon* remains uncertain; character 29; tab.2, fig.20). It is unlikely that the caudally directed fibers of the otic commissure innervate neuromasts, because there are three postotic lateral line nerves whose fibers can be traced to the caudal neuromasts of the sensory canals of the head. In the description of the trigeminal nerve, we noted that some of its sensory fibers penetrate the anterodorsal lateral line ganglion to enter the otic lateral line nerve. We therefore consider it probable that the fibers of the otic commissure are somatosensory fibers arising from the trigeminal nerve (and possibly the facial nerve via its opercular ramus, or, mor; fig.2A). After they anastomose with the middle and supratemporal lateral line nerves, we think that these somatosensory fibers course rostrally in the anterior ramus

of the supratemporal lateral line nerve (a ST; fig.2) to supply the skin overlying the region of the ear.

Having eliminated the otic ramus as part of the facial nerve, then the palatine ramus is the first ramus to arise from the trunk of the facial nerve (pal; fig.2B). The palatine ramus passes ventrally and rostrally and gives rise to its first recognizable ramule at approximately level RC 300. We therefore believe it innervates taste buds and buccal mucosa in the rostral one-third of the buccal cavity, as did Millot and Anthony [1965, fig.26].

The remaining four rami of the facial nerve arise from the hyomandibular trunk as it emerges from the hyomandibular canal: rostrally to caudally, these are 1) the mandibular ramus of the anteroventral lateral line nerve; 2) the mandibular ramus of the facial nerve; 3) the hyoid ramus of the facial nerve, and 4) the opercular ramus of the facial nerve (fig.2). We do not consider the ramus, that innervates neuromasts of the mandibular line (m AV; fig.2), as a component of the facial nerve; rather, we interpret it as the sole component of the anteroventral lateral line nerve (see section on octavolateralis nerves). This component is called the external mandibular ramus of the facial nerve in classical accounts [Norris and Hughes, 1920; Norris, 1925], a conception retained by Millot and Anthony [1965]. While we disagree with their terminology, our observations on the distribution of m AV are in general accord with those of Millot and Anthony, except for their claim that it anastomoses with a ramule of the mandibular ramus of the trigeminal nerve [Millot and Anthony, 1965, p. 61]. Our observations indicate that it is the hyoid ramus of the facial nerve that anastomoses with the mandibular ramus of the trigeminal nerve (v-man + hy; fig.2B).

The mandibular ramus of the facial nerve (m VII; fig. 2B; this is called the internal mandibular ramus of the facial nerve in classical accounts) arises from the hyomandibular trunk, and its course roughly parallels that of the mandibular ramus of the anteroventral lateral line nerve. It innervates the dorsal mucosa and connective tissues of the hyoid arch and the floor of the mouth. In contrast to Millot and Anthony [1965], we find that this ramus divides into two equally sized ramules, which have a convoluted distribution rostrally (dm, vm; fig.2B). Based on their course, we believe these ramules consist only of visceral sensory fibers which ramify as free nerve endings in the mucosa or innervate taste buds associated with the hyoid arch.

The next ramus arising from the hyomandibular trunk is the caudally and laterally directed hyoid ramus, which courses ventral to the hyomandibular cartilage, giving off several caudally directed ramules as indicated by Millot and Anthony [1965, fig.26]. We are uncertain about the components in these ramules, because their caudal continuations are in the region of the gap in the series of sections, but they must contain at least somatic sensory fibers. The hyoid ramus turns rostrally and courses along the lateral surface of the hyoid arch musculature, which it innervates. We also believe the hyoid ramus carries somatic sensory fibers for the adjacent skin.

The most caudal ramus to arise from the hyomandibular trunk is the mixed somatic sensory and motor opercular ramus. Immediately following its origin, a small ventromedially directed ramule innervates the hyomandibular adductor muscle. As the opercular ramus continues caudally, it divides into medial and lateral ramules, which ramify into several elements that innervate the opercular adductor muscle and associated skin. These observations agree with those of Millot and Anthony [1965], however, unlike them, we find that one element of the medial ramule (mor; fig. 2B) turns dorsally and medially to fuse with the anastomosis formed by the otic commissure, the middle lateral line nerve, and the ventral ramus of the supratemporal lateral line nerve (fig. 2A). Given the distribution of elements of the opercular ramus, it must contain sensory fibers and is therefore shown in green in figure 2A. As noted above in our discussion of the otic commissure, somatosensory fibers of the facial nerve may travel this route to innervate the skin overlying the ear.

Except for the anastomoses of elements of the opercular ramus with two of the lateral line nerves, the rami of the facial nerve in *Latimeria* are remarkably similar in their number and distribution to those in elasmobranchs, acipenseriforms, gars, *Amia* and *Ambystoma* [Norris and Hughes, 1920; Norris, 1925; Song and Northcutt, 1991a, b; Northcutt, 1992b]. Thus, the rami of the facial nerve in *Latimeria* appear to conform to the plesiomorphic pattern for gnathostomes (character 20; tab. 2, fig. 20). To explain this pattern, we refer to Norris [1924], who analyzed the serial homology of the various branches of the branchial nerves in gnathostomes. A typical branchial nerve contains a minimum of three rami: 1) a pharyngeal ramus; 2) a pretrematic ramus and 3) a posttrematic ramus. Variation occurs in the branching pattern of the pretrematic and posttrematic rami, although Norris [1924] argued that distinct internal and external pretrematic rami can be distinguished in all gnathostomes. An essential feature of Norris' scheme is the exclusion of all lateralis components from the traditionally recognized branchial nerves. Because we regard the lateralis components as a separate series of cranial nerves, our approach to the branchial nerves is similar. In the case of the facial nerve in *Latimeria*, we exclude from consideration the mandibular ramus of the anteroventral

lateral line nerve; the purely visceral sensory palatine ramus of the facial nerve corresponds to the pharyngeal ramus of a typical branchial nerve; the purely visceral sensory mandibular ramus of the facial nerve corresponds to a pretrematic ramus of a typical branchial nerve; the mixed sensory and motor hyoid ramus corresponds to the posttrematic ramus of a typical branchial nerve; and the mixed sensory and motor opercular ramus corresponds to a dorsal ramus of a typical branchial nerve with the exception of this dorsal sensory ramus; the same general pattern can also be recognized in the glossopharyngeal and vagal nerves of *Latimeria* (characters 36, 38; tab. 2, fig. 20). We also note that the condition in *Polyodon* – which is atypical but which Norris [1924] considered to be a model for gnathostomes – is derived within actinopterygians [Bemis and Grande, unpublished observations]. Thus, the pattern of pharyngeal, pretrematic and posttrematic rami in the facial, glossopharyngeal and vagal nerves of *Latimeria* reflects a synapomorphy of gnathostomes.

Octavolateralis Nerves

A recent resurgence of interest in the organization and evolution of the lateral line nerves [for review, see Northcutt, 1989] has taken two directions: there has been a renewed interest in the development of the lateral line organs and their nerves [Fritzsch and Bolz, 1986; Smith et al., 1988; Northcutt et al., 1990; Northcutt, 1992a]; and modern tracing methods have been used to investigate the innervation of the inner ear and lateral line organs as well as their central projections into the medulla [see Bullock and Heiligenberg, 1986; Coombs et al., 1989; Popper et al., 1992, for review volumes]. Integration of these two approaches will prove especially important to phylogeneticists interested in using characters of the lateral line system in synapomorphy schemes, because it is fundamentally impossible to recognize the homologies of portions of the cranial sensory canals and associated electroreceptor fields without tracing their innervation. So far, combined developmental and tracing studies are available for only a few taxa [e.g. *Ambystoma*, Northcutt, 1992b; *Polyodon*, Bemis and Northcutt, unpublished observations].

Contemporary investigations of the development of the lateral line system proceed from the work of von Kuppfer [1895], Platt [1896], Landacre [1910, 1912, 1916], Coghill [1916] and Stone [1922], whose classical developmental studies established that the sensory organs of the inner ear and lateral line system including electroreceptors, as well as the nerves that innervate these organs, arise from a series of dorsolateral ectodermal placodes. These dorsolateral placodes are separate from the epibranchial placodes [Landacre, 1912] and neural crest, which give rise to the classical branchiomeric cranial nerves. Most research on the development of the cranial nerves occurred 20 years after the comparative anatomical descriptions of the cranial nerves and their components [e.g. Strong, 1895; Herrick, 1899, 1900, 1901; Johnston, 1905]. By the time the major papers were written in the 1920s [e.g. Norris and Hughes, 1920; Norris, 1925], there had been insufficient time to integrate the findings of the developmentalists into the conception of the organization of the lateral line nerves.

As a result, comparative anatomists, with the notable exception of Cole [1896], perpetuated the interpretation that the lateral line nerves are merely components of other cranial nerves. Although contemporary studies rule out that interpretation and instead document the existence of at least six separate lateral line nerves [see reviews by Northcutt, 1989; 1992a; Song and Northcutt, 1991a], these studies came after Millot and Anthony's [1965] description of *Latimeria*. Because Millot and Anthony adhered to previous misinterpretations of the lateral line nerves, we differ almost totally with their account.

Our analysis indicates that *Latimeria* retains three preotic lateral line nerves and three postotic lateral line nerves. The anterodorsal, anteroventral and otic lateral line nerves arise from the brainstem anterior to the ear, whereas the middle, supratemporal and posterior lateral line nerves arise from the brainstem posterior to the ear (characters 21, 25, 27, 30–32; tab. 2, fig. 20).

We discussed above the position of the ganglia of the three preotic lateral line nerves in comparing our account of the trigeminal and facial nerves with that of Millot and Anthony [1965]. Here, we briefly summarize the anatomical relationships of these three nerves and the problems related to their distribution.

All of the craniates listed in table 2 have an anterodorsal lateral line nerve (character 21). All craniates also have two rami of the anterodorsal lateral line nerve, termed the superficial ophthalmic and buccal rami (character 22). In chondrichthyans, there are two separate ganglia located distally in association with the two rami [Cole, 1896; McCready and Boord, 1976]. To our knowledge, all osteichthyans have a single, proximally located ganglion of the anterodorsal lateral line nerve. Because this apparent synapomorphy of osteichthyans needs further comparative study, it is not listed as a character in table 2.

As noted above, the superficial ophthalmic ramus of the anterodorsal lateral line nerve of *Latimeria* is joined by only a few fibers from the trigeminal system and thus *Latimeria* lacks a superficial ophthalmic complex (character 19; tab. 2, fig. 20). Its ramules innervate the neuromasts of the median and supraorbital sensory canals and the putative electroreceptors of the posterior superior and posterior inferior portions of the rostral sac. A short distance after exiting from the neurocranium, the buccal ramus anastomoses with the maxillary ramus of the trigeminal nerve to form the buccal + maxillary complex (character 18; tab. 2, fig. 20). The buccal component of this complex innervates the neuromasts of the preopercular and infraorbital sensory canals as well as the putative electroreceptors of the anterior rostral sac.

Two peculiar aspects of the innervation pattern of the anterodorsal lateral line nerve in *Latimeria* need clarification. The first is its innervation of the neuromasts of the preopercular sensory canal, which, as noted by Millot and Anthony [1965, fig. 52], is unique to *Latimeria* among craniates (character 23; tab. 2, fig. 20). In other gnathostomes, these neuromasts are innervated by the mandibular ramus of the anteroventral lateral line nerve. It is possible that the sensory canal that we interpret as the preopercular canal (fig. 1B) is not homologous to the preopercular canal of other gnathostomes. Alternatively, if this sensory canal is homologous to the preopercular canal of other gnathostomes, then it must be innervated by fibers of the anteroventral lateral line nerve, which enter the buccal ramus via an anterior ramus of the anteroventral lateral line nerve (b AV?; fig. 22B). We are uncertain about this ramus, because we did not observe it in the pup, and the photograph of Millot and Anthony's dissection [1965, plate 3] is unclear. Additional dissections might clarify this, but it is probable that the innervation of the preopercular neuromasts can be resolved only by labeling the buccal ramus to determine whether cell bodies are located in both the anterodorsal and anteroventral lateral line ganglia. In any case, either the innervation of the canal is apomorphic or the canal is apomorphic in *Latimeria*, and this condition may be related to disruption of this region of the head in order to allow bending at the intracranial joint.

The second peculiarity of the anterodorsal lateral line nerve in *Latimeria* is its association with the rostral organ (character 24; tab. 2, fig. 20). Although a rostral organ is clearly present in Devonian coelacanths [Cloutier, 1991], it has not been identified in any other gnathostomes despite attempts to recognize homologues in other groups [Rosen et al., 1981]. It is generally agreed, however, that the rostral organ is an electroreceptive organ as indicated by its structure [Bemis and Hetherington, 1982; Jørgenson, 1991], by the presence of a dorsal octavolateralis nucleus in the medulla [Northcutt, 1980], and by preliminary experiments in the field [Fricke et al., 1987]. Furthermore, histological examination of the skin of the pup and that of adult specimens [Bemis and Hetherington, 1982] reveals no other structures that could be regarded as ampullary electroreceptors. The structure of the rostral organ is consistent with the existence of multiple invagination sites during embryology. In those gnathostomes that have been studied embryologically, the electroreceptors of the snout form along the length of the supraorbital canal and infraorbital canal [*Ambystoma*, Northcutt, 1986; Northcutt et al., 1990; *Polyodon*, Bemis and Northcutt, unpublished observations]. In both of these cases, the supraorbital and infraorbital canals form by rostral elongation of a single v-shaped placode, which we term the anterodorsal lateral line placode. Neuromasts form from each limb of the v, and, subsequently, electroreceptors form from the placodal tissue flanking the lines of neuromasts. The placode gives rise not only to the receptors but also to the ganglion cells of the lateral line nerve that will innervate them, and the outgrowing rami maintain contact with the elongating limbs of the placode. This is probably the plesiomorphic condition for neuromast and electroreceptor development in gnathostomes, although more survey work is needed, so we have not listed it as a character in table 2.

The innervation of the rostral organ of *Latimeria* provides clues regarding its embryology. Specifically, the innervation of the posterior superior and posterior inferior rostral sacs by the supraorbital ramus of the anterodorsal lateral line nerve suggests that these portions of the rostral organ arise from the supraorbital limb of the anterodorsal lateral line placode. The innervation of the anterior rostral sac by the buccal ramus of the anterodorsal lateral line nerve suggests that this portion of the rostral organ arises from the infraorbital limb of the anterodorsal lateral line placode [Northcutt, 1992a; Bemis and Northcutt, unpublished observations].

An anteroventral lateral line nerve is absent in hagfishes but present in lampreys and all gnathostomes (character 25; tab. 2, fig. 20). In *Latimeria*, the ganglion of the anteroventral lateral line nerve is fused with the ganglion of the facial nerve (character 26; tab. 2, fig. 20). We interpret this as a fusion of two separate ganglia, because there is a dorsal population of cells indistinguishable from ganglion cells in other lateral line ganglia, and because there is a separate root of the fused facial + anteroventral ganglion, which joins the ventral root of the anterodorsal lateral line nerve before entering the medulla. We interpret the external mandibular ramus of Millot and Anthony [1965] and classical descriptions [Norris, 1925] to be the sole ramus of the anteroventral lateral line nerve and abbreviate it m AV in

our figures. This ramus innervates the neuromasts of the mandibular sensory canal, and it is the only ramus derived from the fused ganglion to innervate neuromasts. In chondrichthyans and non-teleostean actinopterygians, the ganglion of the anteroventral lateral line nerve is not fused with the facial nerve, and it is frequently closely associated with (or even fused with) the ganglion of the anterodorsal lateral line nerve [Norris and Hughes, 1920; Norris, 1925; McCready and Boord, 1976; Song and Northcutt, 1991a]. For these reasons, we consider the fused condition in *Latimeria* to be apomorphic. An essentially identical fusion occurs in *Ambystoma* [Northcutt, 1992b]. As explained in the discussion of the facial nerve, the condition in lungfishes is somewhat different: all preotic ganglia are fused together. Nevertheless, we adopt the most conservative interpretation and regard character 26 as a synapomorphy of sarcopterygians.

As noted above in the discussion of the facial nerve, the sensory ganglion of the otic lateral line nerve is located immediately adjacent to the ventrolateral border of the ganglion of the anterodorsal lateral line nerve. The ganglion issues rostrally and caudally directed rami, which are the so-called otic rami of the facial nerve of Millot and Anthony [1965] and classical accounts [Norris, 1925]. These rami were discussed under the heading of the facial nerve, but one question concerning their peripheral distribution remains: that is, the nature of a ramule of the posterior ramus, which we were able to trace to the medial wall of the spiracular chamber. We could not identify any structure(s) innervated by this ramus, nor could we identify spiracular organs in the relevant sections of the pup. Examination of better preserved specimens should be made, however, because the presence of spiracular organs is probably a synapomorphy at the level of gnathostomes, and, in all cases, they are innervated by a ramule of the otic lateral line nerve (character 28; tab. 2, fig. 20).

Because the octaval nerve and inner ear lie in the area of 'the gap' in sections from the pup, our knowledge of the distribution of the octaval nerve is incomplete and does not warrant discussion. The description of the ear of *Latimeria* by Millot and Anthony [1965] was supplemented by recent studies of Fritzsch [1987, 1992], who identified features of the ear shared by *Latimeria* and tetrapods.

The middle lateral line nerve is the most rostral of the postotic lateral line nerves. We recognize this nerve based on its distinct ganglion, which occurs immediately caudal to the lateral ganglion of the glossopharyngeal nerve (see section on glossopharyngeal nerve, below). The root of the middle lateral line nerve passes medially and caudally to join the roots of the supratemporal and posterior lateral

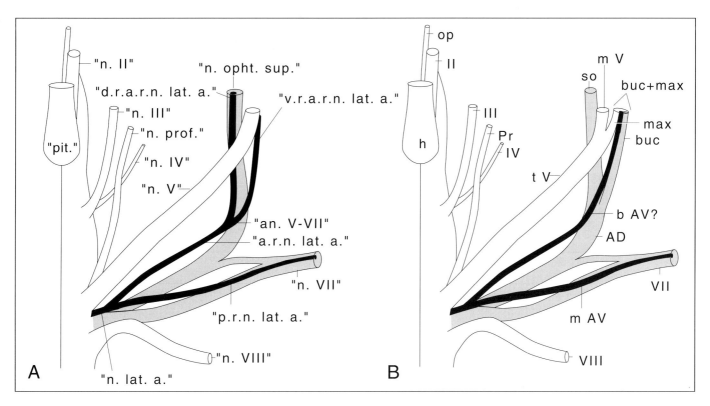

Fig. 22. Reinterpretation of the preotic lateral line nerves. Anterodorsal lateral line nerve in gray; anteroventral lateral line nerve in black. **A** Schematic diagram redrawn from Millot and Anthony [1965, their fig. 17]. Their labeling is retained to facilitate comparison with original. **B** Our reinterpretation labeled according to our nomenclature. See text for explanation. "an. V–VII", anastomosis between trigeminal and facial nerves; "a. r. n. lat. a.", anterior ramus of the anterior lateral line nerve; "d. r. a. r. n. lat. a.", dorsal ramule of the anterior ramus of the anterior lateral line nerve; "n. II", optic nerve; "n. III", oculomotor nerve; "n. prof.", profundal nerve; "n. IV", trochlear nerve; "n. V", trigeminal nerve; "n. opht. sup.", superficial ophthalmic ramus; "n. lat. a.", anterior lateral line nerve; "n. VII", facial nerve; "n. VIII", octaval nerve; "p. r. n. lat. a.", posterior ramus of the anterior lateral line nerve; "pit.", pituitary; "v. r. a. r. n. lat. a.", ventral ramule of the anterior ramus of the anterior lateral line nerve.

line nerves (r POL; fig. 2A). Its only ramus is directed dorsally and laterally to form an anastomosis with components of the otic and supratemporal lateral line nerves and, possibly, cutaneous sensory fibers of the trigeminal and facial nerves. In other gnathostomes, this nerve innervates the neuromasts of the middle pit line and temporal sensory canal [e.g. as in *Lepisosteus*, Song and Northcutt, 1991a; or *Ambystoma*, Northcutt, 1992b]. Because of the anastomoses in this area, we cannot determine which, if any, neuromasts are innervated by the middle lateral line nerve in *Latimeria*, but in all other respects the features of the middle lateral line nerve reflect the general condition for gnathostomes. Although Hensel [1986] revised Millot and Anthony's [1965] description of the pit lines of *Latimeria*, this has not aided our interpretation of the course of the middle lateral line nerve, because it was not accompanied by the necessary retracing of the innervation.

Millot and Anthony [1965, p. 71] recognized a posterior lateral line nerve whose ganglion they described as adhering to the dorsal anterior border of the trunk of the vagal nerve. They noted that the substantial root of this nerve passes rostral to the smaller multiple roots of the vagal nerve to terminate in the medulla. Distally, they recognized an anterior and posterior branch of the nerve proper; they reported that the anterior branch innervates neuromasts of the supratemporal canal and that the posterior branch innervates neuromasts of the posttemporal canal and the trunk canal. Histological examination of this region in the pup confirmed the position and root of the posterior lateral line nerve as described by Millot and Anthony [1965], but we discovered an additional ganglion, closely associated with the dorsal edge of the posterior lateral line ganglion (g ST; fig. 2A). The root of this additional ganglion fuses proximally with the root of the posterior lateral line nerve. The ganglion issues dorsal and ventral rami, which form complex anastomoses with each other and with the otic commissure to produce an anterior ramus that innervates the neuromasts of the supratemporal canal (a ST, fig. 2A). We therefore believe that this ganglion and its processes are homologous to the supratemporal lateral line nerve of other gnathostomes [Song and Northcutt, 1991a]. In other gnathostomes the supratemporal lateral line nerve innervates the neuromasts of the posterior pit line as well as those of the supratemporal canal (character 31; tab. 2, fig. 20). Because of the complex anastomoses in this region of *Latimeria*, it is impossible to establish the precise innervation of the neuromasts without applying modern tracing techniques. Our current interpretation is that the supratemporal lateral line nerve is plesiomorphic to gnathostomes, and possibly a synapomorphy of craniates.

In their description of the caudal continuation of the posterior lateral line nerve, Millot and Anthony [1965] noted that it passes lateral to the lateral ganglion of the vagal nerve and gives rise to: a lateral ramule, which innervates the first two or three neuromasts of the trunk; a small dorsal ramus (termed the 'accessory lateral nerve' by Millot and Anthony [1965, fig. 36]); and a larger main trunk nerve. We recognize Millot and Anthony's three divisions of the posterior lateral line nerve, but we differ in our interpretation of their accessory lateral line nerve, which we recognize as the dorsal ramus of the posterior lateral line nerve. Millot and Anthony [1965, p. 72] postulated that the small ramules issued from the dorsal ramus, innervate taste buds located in the skin of the trunk. We believe that this is unlikely, as all superficial taste buds on the trunk in fishes investigated thus far are innervated by a recurrent branch of the facial nerve [Herrick, 1901; Finger, 1983]. We consider it more likely that the dorsal ramus innervates free neuromasts of a dorsal trunk line, but the material available is insufficient to resolve this point. In any event, the presence of a dorsal ramus of the posterior lateral line nerve is plesiomorphic for gnathostomes, and possibly a synapomorphy of myopterygians (character 33; tab. 2, fig. 20).

A ventral ramus of the posterior lateral line nerve is absent in *Latimeria*. When present, this ramus innervates a line of superficial neuromasts low on the trunk [e.g. as in lungfishes and amphibians, Northcutt, 1992b]. This ramus and the neuromasts it innervates have an interesting phylogenetic distribution, being found in neonatal elasmobranchs, lungfishes, amphibians, and possibly lampreys but not in any basal actinopterygian. Its absence in *Latimeria* appears to be apomorphic for coelacanths (character 34; tab. 2, fig. 20).

Glossopharyngeal Nerve

Millot and Anthony's [1965] analysis of the glossopharyngeal nerve is confounded by their interpretation that it possesses a lateralis component. Because they had no histological preparations, they failed to detect an additional small ganglion immediately caudal to the lateral ganglion of the glossopharyngeal nerve; we interpret this small ganglion as the sensory ganglion of the middle lateral line nerve (g MLLN; fig. 2A). Millot and Anthony [1965] described what we interpret as the root of the middle lateral line nerve, which is also figured in two of their diagrams (intracranially as a dashed but unlabeled component of IX in their fig. 17 and extracranially as a rostral unlabeled root of IX in their fig. 31). In the pup, the root of the middle lateral line nerve passes along the caudal edge of the medial ganglion of the glossopharyngeal nerve and turns caudally to fuse with the roots of the supratemporal and posterior lateral line nerves (dashed lines in fig. 2A). We interpret this root as comprising the centrally directed axons of the ganglion of the middle lateral line nerve. Millot and Anthony [1965] were thus incorrect in assuming that this root carries lateralis fibers from the posterior lateral line nerve to the glossopharyngeal nerve. Millot and Anthony [1965] also described a fine ascending ramus rising from the glossopharyngeal nerve to innervate the adjacent integument. We found this ramus, but it actually arises from the middle lateral line nerve ganglion and joins the anastomosis of the otic commissure, the opercular ramus of the facial nerve, and the supratemporal lateral line nerve. Ramules from this anastomosis innervate neuromasts of the temporal canal, which in other anamniotic gnathostomes are innervated by the middle lateral line nerve, so we conclude that *Latimeria* exhibits a synapomorphy at the level of myopterygians (character 30; tab. 2, fig. 20).

Returning to the glossopharyngeal nerve proper, we note that, like in most tetrapods, it exhibits both medial and lateral sensory ganglia (character 35; tab. 2, fig. 20). Like the facial nerve discussed above, the pattern of peripheral rami of the glossopharyngeal nerve in *Latimeria* is conservative, presumably reflecting a synapomorphy of gnathostomes (character 36; tab. 2, fig. 20). Like Millot and Anthony [1965, fig. 31], we find that two major branches arise from the distal pole of the lateral ganglion of the glossopharyngeal nerve. The anterior branch is a common trunk for the pharyngeal and pretrematic rami (fig. 2B, 18). The pharyngeal ramus (p IX; fig. 18) passes rostrally to supply the mucosa of the middle one-third of the buccal cavity; it is entirely sensory, ramifying as free nerve endings and supplying the taste buds of that region. The single pretrematic ramus also passes rostrally and courses along the medial edge of the hyomandibula to innervate the lamellae of the hyoid hemibranch (pr IX; fig. 18). We corroborate Millot and Anthony's [1965] description of these two rami, but note that they termed our pharyngeal ramus 'the internal ramus' and our pretrematic ramus 'the external ramus'.

In our material we have not seen any branch of the glossopharyngeal nerve that could be interpreted as a dorsal somatosensory ramus innervating the skin. This is important, because a dorsal somatosensory ramus is considered part of a typical branchial nerve in fishes, as proposed by Allis [1920], although Norris [1924] denied that a dorsal sensory ramus exists as a typical feature. Unfortunately, Allis' [1920] conception has entered the literature as 'the typical branchial nerve' [e.g. see Romer, 1972]. The inclusion of a dorsal somatosensory ramus in the model of a 'typical branchial nerve' is almost certainly an error resulting from misinterpretations of the closely associated rami of the lateral line nerves.

The posterior branch of the glossopharyngeal ganglion is the posttrematic ramus of the glossopharyngeal nerve. Our description (fig. 18) of the branching of the posttrematic ramus differs in several respects from that of Millot and Anthony [1965, fig. 31], and they neither illustrated nor described the detailed subdivisions of the ramus as it enters the gill arch. Comparison of the branching pattern of the glossopharyngeal nerve in *Latimeria* with the branching pattern in other vertebrates [Norris, 1924, 1925] suggests that *Latimeria* retains the branching pattern found in gnathostomes generally. The exclusively sensory pharyngeal ramus of the glossopharyngeal nerve (p IX, fig. 2A, 18) corresponds to the pharyngeal ramus of a typical branchial nerve. Unlike the pattern reported in *Polyodon* by Norris [1924, 1925], the glossopharyngeal nerve in *Latimeria* has only a single pretrematic ramus, but this condition is probably plesiomorphic for gnathostomes, as noted above in the discussion of the facial nerve. Finally, it is possible to distinguish two major ramules of the posttrematic ramus that correspond with ramules identified by Norris [1924] in *Polyodon*. Our dorsal ramule of the posttrematic ramus of the glossopharyngeal nerve (dr IX, fig. 18) corresponds to the internal posttrematic ramule of *Polyodon* [Norris, 1924, fig. 1]. Our ventral ramule of the posttrematic ramus of the glossopharyngeal nerve (vr IX, fig. 18) corresponds to the posterior posttrematic ramule in *Polyodon* [Norris, 1924, fig. 1], and our first pretrematic ramus of the vagal nerve (1pr X, fig. 18) corresponds to the external pretrematic ramus in *Polyodon* [Norris, 1924]. The various subdivisions and fusions of these ramules that take place within the gill arch are essentially similar to those reported for the poste-

rior posttrematic ramus and external pretrematic ramus of typical branchial nerves as figured by Norris [1924, fig. 1–4].

Vagal Nerve

As noted in the Results section, we have incomplete information about the branches of the vagal nerve. To the extent that the material allows, however, we can comment on differences between our observations and those of Millot and Anthony [1965]. Our reconstruction of the roots and ganglia of the vagal nerve is complete and indicates that, as in the glossopharyngeal nerve, medial and lateral sensory ganglia can be recognized (mg X, lg X; fig. 2B); separate ganglia were not noted by Millot and Anthony [1965], but their presence may be a synapomorphy of osteichthyans (character 37; tab. 2, fig. 20). Like Millot and Anthony [1965, p. 66], we recognize three branchial trunks and a visceral trunk leaving the lateral ganglion in rostral to caudal sequence. Our reconstruction of the first and second branchial trunks is essentially complete, but the series of sections ends at the level of the divergence of the third branchial trunk from the visceral trunk. Therefore we cannot comment on the innervation of the fourth and fifth gill arches or of the viscera.

Our description of the first branchial trunk of the vagal nerve differs considerable from that of Millot and Anthony [1965]. First, there is apparently a crucial printing error in their account (p. 66, right hand column, last paragraph), in which 'La branche postérieure' should read 'La branche antérieure'. This is the branch that we term the first branchial trunk of the vagal nerve (it is abbreviated in Millot and Anthony's fig. 31 as 'n. X, br. a.'). Much of the confusion surrounding this trunk results from their belief that it provides motor innervation to the basicranial muscle. They claimed that as the first branchial trunk is traced ventrally and laterally it first gives rise to a pharyngeal ramus which passes deep to the levator of arch 1 and is shown ramifying ventral to the basicranial muscle (this ramus is Millot and Anthony's [1965] n. ph., fig. 31, but it is not listed in their list of abbreviations). According to their description, the next distal ramus of the first branchial trunk is the 'nerf du muscle sous-crânien', which they diagram as 'n. sousc.' in figure 31 (this is also omitted from their list of abbreviations). The continuation of this first branchial trunk they interpret as a posttrematic ramus (not labeled in their fig. 31). Millot and Anthony [1965] thus considered that the first branchial trunk of the vagal nerve lacked a pretrematic ramus.

It is clear from our reconstruction and details published elsewhere [Bemis and Northcutt, 1991] that the basicranial muscle of *Latimeria* is innervated by the abducent nerve. Furthermore, we found distinct pharyngeal and pretrematic rami arising from the common first branchial trunk, which arises from the rostral pole of the lateral sensory ganglion of the vagal nerve (the subsequent branches of the pharyngeal ramus of the first branchial trunk of the vagal nerve are indicated by m1p X and l1p X, fig. 2B; the pretrematic ramus is indicated by 1pr X, fig. 2B, 18). The ramus that Millot and Anthony [1965] interpreted as the 'nerf du muscle sous-crânien' is clearly the pharyngeal ramus of the first branchial trunk of the vagal nerve. It would have been easy to misinterpret this ramus in a dissection, but it is clear from histological examination that the ramus ramifies only in the mucosa overlying the basicranial muscle and does not actually enter the muscle itself. With this fact established, the ramus that they interpreted as the first pharyngeal ramus ['n. ph.', Millot and Anthony, 1965, their fig. 31] must be considered the pretrematic ramus of the first branchial trunk of the vagal nerve. In fact, we traced this ramus in histological sections into the glossopharyngeal arch, exactly where the first pretrematic of the vagal nerve should go (1pr X; fig. 18). As far as we can determine, the subsequent course of the first posttrematic ramus of the vagal nerve is identical to that of the posttrematic ramus of the glossopharyngeal nerve (fig. 2B, 18).

The pharyngeal rami of the first, second, and third vagal trunks [see Millot and Anthony, 1965, fig. 31, for the distribution of the third pharyngeal ramus of the vagal nerve] course ventrally and rostrally to innervate the caudal one-third of the mucosa of the oral cavity and pharynx.

The second branchial trunk of the vagal nerve is termed the middle trunk by Millot and Anthony [1965, fig. 31, 'n. X, br. m.'] and arises midventrally from the lateral vagal ganglion in a manner similar to that of the first branchial trunk. Although we can clearly recognize the origin of the second pretrematic ramus, the existing sections did not extend far enough to allow us to identify the second posttrematic ramus. Caudally, we can establish only that a third branchial trunk and visceral trunk arise from the caudal pole of the lateral ganglion, essentially as reported by Millot and Anthony [1965, fig. 31, 'n. X, br. p' and 'r. intest. br. p.'].

Although we have described these ganglia and their rami as components of the vagal nerve, recent developments in the comparative anatomy of the spinal accessory nerve of skates [Boord and Sperry, 1991] demonstrate that the classical vagal nerve of elasmobranchs also carries motor fibers that travel in the spinal accessory nerve of amniotes. We did not recognize homologues of the trapezius muscle in *Latimeria*, nor were we able to trace components of the vagal nerve that might be homologues of the spinal accessory nerve. Nevertheless, what we have described in *Latimeria* as the vagal nerve almost certainly contains fibers that would travel in the spinal accessory nerve of anamniotes.

Phylogenetically, the three branchial trunks of the vagal nerve – particularly the first trunk – correspond to the branching pattern expected for typical branchial nerves. As noted in the discussion of the octavolateralis nerves (above), we recognize separate supratemporal and posterior lateral line nerves, which are independent anatomically and phylogenetically from the vagal nerve. We did not observe any dorsal somatosensory rami of the glossopharyngeal or vagal nerves innervating the skin of the posterior dorsal surface of the head in *Latimeria*. As explained above, we consider that this area of the skin is innervated by fibers of the trigeminal or facial nerves, which reach their destinations via the anastomosis that we term the otic commissure (oc, fig. 2). The absence of dorsal sensory rami in the glossopharyngeal and vagal nerves is probably the ancestral condition for gnathostomes, but more survey is needed. The occurrence of the pharyngeal rami of the vagal trunks is also typical and presumably a retention of a synapomorphy of gnathostomes. Moreover, as noted above in the discussion of the glossopharyngeal nerve, the occurrence of a single pretrematic ramus in *Latimeria* is also a retention of a gnathostome synapomorphy (as opposed to the internal and external pretrematic rami said to be typical of branchial nerves by Norris [1924]. Finally, we noted there is nothing unusual about the posttrematic rami of the vagal trunks insofar as we can tell, and their distribution along the anterior and posterior surfaces of the gill arches (internal posttrematic and posterior posttrematic, respectively, of Norris [1924] is likely to be similar to gnathostomes generally.

Occipital Nerves

The course of the occipital nerves could not be determined in the pup, but we agree with Millot and Anthony [1965, fig. 34] that there are three occipital nerves. This pattern may be the ancestral condition for gnathostomes, but it must be more completely surveyed before listing it as a character.

General Conclusions

Although the cranial nerves of *Latimeria* exhibit a number of autapomorphies, the basic pattern of the nerves is very conservative. For example, among the thirty-eight characters scored, *Latimeria* shares six synapomorphies at the level of craniates, an additional ten at the level of myopterygians, and seven more at the level of gnathostomes. Among its autapomorphies, we cannot readily explain the absence of a terminal nerve in *Latimeria*. Two autapomorphies of the nerves of *Latimeria* relate to the rostral organ, which is probably a synapomorphy for coelacanths. Additional characters, such as the unusual innervation of the preopercular line, may be related to the function of the basicranial joint. At present there is insufficient evidence to determine whether the basicranial joint and muscles were present in the common ancestor of all bony fishes, as interpreted by Bjerring [1973]; however, we consider that these features are more likely derived at some level within Sarcopterygii and identify the basicranial muscle as a putative synapomorphy of *Latimeria* and tetrapods.

Characters of the cranial nerves have been incorporated into few phylogenetic analyses. Because these characters are so conservative, they should be most useful at high phylogenetic levels, and, like slowly evolving molecules, may prove important for studying broad patterns in vertebrate phylogeny. The discovery and use of these characters awaits consistent and careful comparisons using histology and modern tracing methods to study the cranial ganglia. Some interesting phylogenetic questions that stem directly from this work include: what is the phylogenetic distribution of dorsal sensory branches of the branchiomeric nerves? Is the superficial ophthalmic ramus of the trigeminal nerve a plesiomorphic feature of craniates, or is its well-developed condition in amniotes apomorphic? What are the varying patterns of fusion of the profundal and trigeminal ganglia among sarcopterygians and tetrapods? It may be impossible to exceed in quality or impact the work of Allis [1889], Herrick [1899], Johnston [1905] and Norris [1925], but we still need clear, modern studies of the cranial nerves for most groups of craniates, particularly hagfishes and lampreys. Finally, embryological studies are central to future comparative research on cranial nerves, particularly if we are to understand phylogenetic differences among those systems derived from dorsolateral placodes, epibranchial placodes, and neural crest.

Summary

We reconstructed the cranial nerves of a serially sectioned prenatal coelacanth, *Latimeria chalumnae*. This allowed us to correct several mistakes in the literature and to make broad phylogenetic comparisons with other craniates. The genera surveyed in our phylogenetic analysis were *Eptatretus*, *Myxine*, *Petromyzon*, *Lampetra*, *Chimaera*, *Hydrolagus*, *Squalus*, *Mustelus*, *Polypterus*, *Acipenser*, *Lepisosteus*, *Amia*, *Neoceratodus*, *Protopterus*, *Lepidosiren*, *Latimeria* and *Ambystoma*. Cladistic analysis of our data shows that *Latimeria* shares with *Ambystoma* two characters of the cranial nerves. Our chief findings are:

1) *Latimeria* possesses an external nasal papilla and pedunculated olfactory bulbs but lacks a discrete terminal nerve. In other respects its olfactory system resembles the plesiomorphic pattern for craniates.

2) The optic nerve is plicated, a character found in many but not all gnathostomes. *Latimeria* retains an interdigitated partial decussation of the optic nerves, a character found in all craniates surveyed.

3) The oculomotor nerve supplies the same extrinsic eye muscles as in lampreys and gnathostomes. As in gnathostomes generally, *Latimeria* has a ciliary ganglion but its cells are located intracranially in the root of the oculomotor nerve, and their processes reach the eye via oculomotor and profundal rami.

4) The trochlear nerve supplies the superior oblique muscle as in all craniates that have not secondarily reduced the eye and its extrinsic musculature.

5) The profundal ganglion and ramus are entirely separate from the trigeminal system, with no exchange of fibers. This character has an interesting phylogenetic distribution: in hagfishes, lampreys, lungfishes and tetrapods, the profundal and trigeminal ganglia are fused, whereas in other taxa surveyed the ganglia are separate. The principal tissues innervated by the profundal nerve are the membranous walls of the tubes of the rostral organ.

6) As in lampreys and gnathostomes, the trigeminal nerve has maxillary and mandibular rami. Unlike all other gnathostomes surveyed, the trigeminal nerve of *Latimeria* lacks a sizable superficial ophthalmic ramus. Thus, *Latimeria* lacks the well-developed superficial ophthalmic complex reported in most other fishes. As in gnathostomes generally, the maxillary ramus of the trigeminal nerve fuses with the buccal ramus of the anterodorsal lateral line nerve to form the buccal + maxillary complex. We reject the term 'Gasserian ganglion', which is often applied to the fused profundal and trigeminal ganglion of tetrapods.

7) The abducent nerve innervates not only the lateral rectus muscle (a character common to myopterygians) but also the basicranial muscle. As we previously reported, it is probable that the basicranial muscle of *Latimeria* is homologous to the ocular retracter muscle of amphibians.

8) As in all craniates surveyed, *Latimeria* has an anterodorsal lateral line nerve (ADLLN). As in myopterygians, the ADLLN has superficial ophthalmic and buccal rami; the condition in hagfishes is not clear. The putative electroreceptive epithelium of the rostral organ (an organ unique to coelacanths) is innervated by the ADLLN. The sensory crypts associated with the posterior superior and posterior inferior tubes of the rostral organ are innervated by the superficial ophthalmic ramus of the ADLLN. The sensory crypts associated with the anterior tube of the rostral organ are innervated by the buccal ramus of the ADLLN. Also, the buccal ramus of the ADLLN innervates not only neuromasts of the infraorbital line but also some neuromasts of the preopercular line, an unusual distribution pattern for this ramus that may be related to the presence of the intracranial joint in *Latimeria*.

9) *Latimeria* shares with myopterygians the presence of an anteroventral lateral line nerve (AVLLN). The ganglion of the AVLLN is fused to that of the facial nerve. We find compelling evidence based on the size and distribution

of cell bodies in the fused ganglion that the AVLLN should be regarded as a separate cranial nerve in *Latimeria*. The phylogenetic distribution of this fusion suggests that it is a synapomorphy of sarcopterygians. The anteroventral lateral line nerve in other vertebrates normally innervates all neuromasts of the preopercular and mandibular sensory lines, but as noted in finding number 8 (above), this responsibility is shared with the buccal ramus of the anterodorsal lateral line nerve in *Latimeria*.

10) If the lateralis components are removed from consideration, then the facial nerve is recognized to have: a palatine ramus (equivalent to the pharyngeal ramus of a typical branchial nerve); a mandibular ramus (equivalent to the pretrematic ramus of a typical branchial nerve); a hyoid ramus (equivalent to the posttrematic ramus of a typical branchial nerve); as well as dorsal sensory components. In these respects, the facial nerve conforms to ideas about 'typical' branchial nerves of gnathostomes.

11) As in many gnathostomes studied carefully to date, *Latimeria* has a separate otic lateral line nerve innervating neuromasts of the otic sensory canal. There is also a spiracular ramus of the otic lateral line nerve – but no clearly identifiable spiracular organ – in *Latimeria*. These two characters are difficult to evaluate in lampreys, but are certainly absent in hagfishes. *Latimeria* also has an unusual anastomosis that we term the otic commissure among portions of the otic, middle and supratemporal nerves and which we interpret as a route for somatic sensory fibers of the facial or trigeminal nerves to reach the skin of the posterodorsal region of the head.

12) There are three postotic lateral line nerves. The first is the middle lateral line nerve (MLLN), previously unreported for *Latimeria*, but probably a plesiomorphic feature of gnathostomes and possibly present in lampreys. Second, there is a discrete supratemporal lateral line nerve (STLLN). We consider that the STLLN may be present in all craniates. The supratemporal ganglion is closely associated with but clearly separable from that of the posterior lateral line nerve (PLLN), which is the third and largest postotic lateral line nerve. The PLLN is present in myopterygians. In those taxa with all three of the postotic lateral line nerves there is a common root entering the medulla.

13) The glossopharyngeal nerve of *Latimeria* has medial and lateral ganglia, a character found only in *Latimeria* among the taxa surveyed but present in most tetrapods. Pharyngeal, pretrematic and posttrematic rami of IX are present, a pattern plesiomorphic for gnathostomes. Significantly, the glossopharyngeal and vagal nerves of *Latimeria* lack dorsal somatic rami for the overlying skin, and in this respect, they differ from classical interpretations of 'typical'

branchial nerves. The condition of dorsal somatic rami of IX and X needs to be examined by a modern comparative study.

14) Our interpretation of the peripheral distribution of the vagal nerve differs from previous accounts, chiefly in that no vagal fibers innervate the basicranial muscle and that the first vagal trunk has a pretrematic ramus. Like the glossopharyngeal nerve, the vagal nerve of *Latimeria* has medial and lateral sensory ganglia, and its branchial trunks have pharyngeal, pretrematic and posttrematic rami. Our phylogenetic survey suggests that the presence of medial and lateral sensory ganglia of X is a synapomorphy of osteichthyans.

Our comparative analysis indicates that *Latimeria* retains many features of the cranial nerves that are synapomorphies at the level of craniates or gnathostomes. This extreme conservatism with respect to ganglia, entering roots, and peripheral rami means that we expect and must look carefully for common development patterns of the cranial nerves throughout craniates. The most interesting potential synapomorphies discovered by our comparative analysis are those of lampreys and gnathostomes. Most of the autapomorphic features that we discovered in *Latimeria* are related to unusual organs (e.g., the rostral organ). There are, however, some autapomorphies of *Latimeria*, such as the absence of a terminal nerve, which are more difficult to understand. Several characters with potentially interesting phylogenetic distributions were omitted from our analysis because the conditions in many taxa are inadequately known. For these reasons, we hope that our study of *Latimeria* provokes future work on the comparative anatomy and development of cranial nerves as well as tracing of nerve components using modern techniques.

Appendix

List of sections of AMNH 32949h, embryo 1 in rostral to caudal (RC) sequence correlated with previous numbering schemes

RC number[1]	Packet number[2]	Ink number[3]	Slide size[4]	Comments[5]	RC number[1]	Packet number[2]	Ink number[3]	Slide size[4]	Comments[5]
RC 1	A6 549	1	lantern		RC 24	A6 521	24		
RC 2	A6 548	2			RC 25	A6 519	25	lantern	
RC 3	A6 547	3			RC 26	A6 518	26		
RC 4	A6 546	4			RC 27	A6 517	27		
RC 5	A6 544	5			RC 28	A6 516	28		
RC 6	A6 543	6			RC 29	A6 515	29		
RC 7	A6 542	7			RC 30	A6 514	30	lantern	
RC 8	A6 541	8			RC 31	A6 513	31		
RC 9	A6 539	9	lantern		RC 32	A6 512	32		
RC 10	A6 538	10			RC 33	A6 511	33		
RC 11	A6 537	11			RC 34	A6 510	34	lantern	
RC 12	A6 536	12			RC 35	A6 509	35		
RC 13	A6 534	13			RC 36	A6 508	36		
RC 14	A6 532	14			RC 37	A6 507	37		
RC 15	A6 531	15	lantern		RC 38	A6 506	38		
RC 16	A6 530	16	lantern		RC 39	A6 505	39		
RC 17	A6 528	17			RC 40	A6 505	40	lantern	Duplicate No. A6 505
RC 18	A6 527	18			RC 41	A6 504	41		
RC 19	A6 526	19			RC 42	A6 502	42		
RC 20	A6 525	20			RC 43	A6 501	43		
RC 21	A6 524	21	lantern		RC 44	A6 500	44	lantern	
RC 22	A6 523	22			RC 45	A5 499	45		
RC 23	A6 522	23			RC 46	A5 498	46		

[1]   The sections were cut, stained and mounted in the laboratory of M. Lagios. They were placed in rostral to caudal (RC) order and double checked before paper labels with RC numbers were placed on the slides.

[2]   This is an obsolete set of numbers written on each slide by the original processors; we refer to them as 'Packet Numbers'; they are typed, and consist of a packet letter followed by the number. Many of these numbers were inadvertently duplicated during transcription, as indicated under the 'Comments' column.

[3]   This is an obsolete set of numbers written in ink and thus referred to as 'Ink Numbers'. They presumably represent an earlier attempt to correctly order the slides.

[4]   If not indicated in this column, then the section was mounted on a standard 2″×3″ (51 mm×76 mm) slide. Some of the sections were mounted on 3.25″×4″ (83 mm×102 mm) lantern slides. The two series of slides are stored in separate boxes.

[5]   Many of the sections were mounted upside down. This was corrected by placing red paper dots in a standard corner on every slide. When holding a slide so that the red dot is in its lower right corner, dorsal is to the top of the slide and the anatomical left side of the specimen is towards the right.

RC number[1]	Packet number[2]	Ink number[3]	Slide size[4]	Comments[5]	RC number[1]	Packet number[2]	Ink number[3]	Slide size[4]	Comments[5]
RC 47	A5 497	47	lantern		RC 102	A5 441	102		
RC 48	A5 496	48			RC 103	A5 440	103	lantern	
RC 49	A5 495	49			RC 104	A5 439	104		
RC 50	A5 453	90			RC 105	A5 438	105		
RC 51	A5 493	51			RC 106	A5 437	106		
RC 52	A5 492	52	lantern		RC 107	A5 436	107		
RC 53	A5 491	53			RC 108	A5 435	108	lantern	
RC 54	A5 490	54			RC 109	A5 434	109		
RC 55	A5 480	63			RC 110	A5 433	110		
RC 56	A5 488	56			RC 111	A5 432	111		
RC 57	A5 485	57	lantern		RC 112	A5 431	112		
RC 58	A5 484	58			RC 113	A5 430	113	lantern	
RC 59	A5 483	59			RC 114	A5 429	114		
RC 60	A5 482	60			RC 115	A5 428	115		
RC 61	A5 481	61	lantern	Duplicate No. A5 481	RC 116	A5 427	116		
RC 62	A5 481	62			RC 117	A5 426	117		
RC 63	A5 489	55			RC 118	A5 425	118	lantern	
RC 64	A5 478	64			RC 119	A5 424	119		
RC 65	A5 477	65			RC 120	A5 423	120		
RC 66	A5 476	66			RC 121	A5 422	121		
RC 67	A5 475	67	lantern		RC 122	A5 421	122		
RC 68	A5 474	68			RC 123	A5 420	123	lantern	
RC 69	A5 473	69			RC 124	A5 419	124		
RC 70	A5 472	70			RC 125	A5 418	125		
RC 71	A5 471	71			RC 126	A5 417	126		
RC 72	A5 460	82			RC 127	A5 416	127		
RC 73	A5 470	72	lantern		RC 128	A5 415	128	lantern	
RC 74	A5 469	73			RC 129	A5 414	129		
RC 75	A5 468	74			RC 130	A5 413	130		
RC 76	A5 467	75			RC 131	A5 412	131		
RC 77	A5 466	76	lantern		RC 132	A5 410	132	lantern	
RC 78	A5 465	77			RC 133	A5 409	133		
RC 79	A5 464	78			RC 134	A5 408	134		
RC 80	A5 463	79			RC 135	A5 407	135		
RC 81	A5 462	80			RC 136	A5 406	136		
RC 82	A5 461	81			RC 137	A5 405	137	lantern	
RC 83	A5 460	83	lantern	Duplicate No. A5 460	RC 138	A5 404	138		
RC 84	A5 459	84			RC 139	A5 403	139		
RC 85	A5 458	85			RC 140	A5 402	140		
RC 86	A5 457	86			RC 141	A5 401	141		
RC 87	A5 456	87			RC 142	A5 400	142	lantern	
RC 88	A5 455	88	lantern		RC 143	A4 399	236		
RC 89	A5 454	89			RC 144	A4 398	235		
RC 90	A5 494	50			RC 145	A4 397	234		
RC 91	A5 452	91			RC 146	A4 395	232	lantern	
RC 92	A5 451	92			RC 147	A4 396	233		
RC 93	A5 450	93	lantern		RC 148	A4 400	237		
RC 94	A5 449	94			RC 149	A4 393	231		
RC 95	A5 448	95			RC 150	A4 392	230		
RC 96	A5 447	96			RC 151	A4 391	229		
RC 97	A5 446	97			RC 152	A4 390	228	lantern	Duplicate No. A4 390
RC 98	A5 445	98	lantern		RC 153	A4 389	226		
RC 99	A5 444	99			RC 154	A4 388	225		
RC 100	A5 443	100			RC 155	A4 387	224		
RC 101	A5 442	101			RC 156	A4 388	223	lantern	

RC number[1]	Packet number[2]	Ink number[3]	Slide size[4]	Comments[5]	RC number[1]	Packet number[2]	Ink number[3]	Slide size[4]	Comments[5]
RC 157	A4 384	222			RC 212	A4 328	168		
RC 158	A4 390	227			RC 213	A4 327	167		
RC 159	A4 383	221			RC 214	A4 326	166		
RC 160	A4 382	220			RC 215	A4 325	165	lantern	
RC 161	A4 381	219			RC 216	A4 324	164		
RC 162	A4 380	218	lantern		RC 217	A4 323	163		
RC 163	A4 379	217			RC 218	A4 322	162		
RC 164	A4 378	216			RC 219	A4 321	161		
RC 165	A4 376	214			RC 220	A4 320	160	lantern	
RC 166	A4 375	213	lantern		RC 221	A4 319	159		
RC 167	A4 367	205			RC 222	A4 310	152		
RC 168	A4 374	212			RC 223	A4 316	158		
RC 169	A4 373	211			RC 224	A4 314	157		
RC 170	A4 372	210			RC 225	A4 313	156		
RC 171	A4 371	209			RC 226	A4 312	155		
RC 172	A4 368	206			RC 227	A4 311	154		
RC 173	A4 370	208	lantern		RC 228	A4 310	153	lantern	Duplicate No. A4 310
RC 174	A4 369	207	lantern		RC 229	A4 309	151		
RC 175	A4 377	215			RC 230	A4 308	150		
RC 176	A4 366	204			RC 231	A4 307	149		
RC 177	A4 365	203	lantern		RC 232	A4 306	148		
RC 178	A4 364	202			RC 233	A4 305	147	lantern	
RC 179	A4 363	201			RC 234	A4 304	146		
RC 180	A4 362	200			RC 235	A4 303	145		
RC 181	A4 361	199			RC 236	A4 301	143		
RC 182	A4 360	198	lantern		RC 237	A4 302	144	lantern	
RC 183	A4 359	197	lantern		RC 238	A3 300	326		
RC 184	A4 359	196			RC 239	A3 299	325	lantern	
RC 185	A4 352	191			RC 240	A3 298	324		
RC 186	A4 355	194	lantern		RC 241	A3 297	323		
RC 187	A4 354	193			RC 242	A3 296	322		
RC 188	A4 353	192			RC 243	A3 295	321	lantern	
RC 189	A4 356	195			RC 244	A3 294	320		
RC 190	A4 351	190			RC 245	A3 293	319		
RC 191	A4 350	189	lantern		RC 246	A3 292	318		
RC 192	A4 349	188			RC 247	A3 291	317		
RC 193	A4 348	187			RC 248	A3 290	316	lantern	
RC 194	A4 347	186			RC 249	A3 289	315		
RC 195	A4 346	185			RC 250	A3 286	313		Folded section
RC 196	A4 345	184	lantern		RC 251	A3 283	310		
RC 197	A4 344	183			RC 252	A3 285	312	lantern	
RC 198	A4 343	182			RC 253	A3 284	311		
RC 199	A4 342	181			RC 254	A3 280	309		
RC 200	A4 341	180			RC 255	A3 288	314		
RC 201	A4 340	179	lantern		RC 256	A3 280	308	lantern	Duplicate No. A3 280
RC 202	A4 339	178			RC 257	A3 279	307		
RC 203	A4 338	177			RC 258	A3 278	306		
RC 204	A4 337	176			RC 259	A3 277	305		
RC 205	A4 336	175			RC 260	A3 276	304		
RC 206	A4 335	174	lantern		RC 261	A3 275	303	lantern	
RC 207	A4 334	173			RC 262	A3 274	302		
RC 208	A4 333	172			RC 263	A3 273	301		
RC 209	A4 332	171			RC 264	A3 272	300		
RC 210	A4 331	170			RC 265	A3 270	299		
RC 211	A4 330	169	lantern		RC 266	A3 270	298	lantern	Duplicate No. A3 270

RC number[1]	Packet number[2]	Ink number[3]	Slide size[4]	Comments[5]	RC number[1]	Packet number[2]	Ink number[3]	Slide size[4]	Comments[5]
RC 267	A3 269	297			RC 322	A3 210	242		
RC 268	A3 268	296			RC 323	A3 210	241	lantern	Duplicate No. A3 210
RC 269	A3 267	295			RC 324	A3 204	240	lantern	
RC 270	A3 266	294			RC 325	A3 203	239		
RC 271	A3 265	293			RC 326	A3 200	238	lantern	
RC 272	A3 264	292	lantern		RC 327	A2 199	398		
RC 273	A3 263	291			RC 328	A2 198	397	lantern	
RC 274	A3 262	290			RC 329	A2 196	396		
RC 275	A3 260	289			RC 330	A2 194	395	lantern	
RC 276	A3 260	288	lantern	Duplicate No. A3 260	RC 331	A2 193	394		
RC 277	A3 259	287			RC 332	A2 191	393		
RC 278	A3 258	286			RC 333	A2 190	392	lantern	Duplicate No. A2 190
RC 279	A3 257	285			RC 334	A2 189	390		
RC 280	A3 256	284			RC 335	A2 188	389		
RC 281	A3 255	283			RC 336	A2 187	388		
RC 282	A3 254	282			RC 337	A2 186	387		
RC 283	A3 253	281	lantern		RC 338	A2 185	386	lantern	
RC 284	A3 251	280			RC 339	A2 184	385		
RC 285	A3 250	279	lantern		RC 340	A2 183	384		
RC 286	A3 249	278			RC 341	A2 182	383		
RC 287	A3 248	277	lantern		RC 342	A2 190	391		
RC 288	A3 247	276			RC 343	A2 180	382	lantern	
RC 289	A3 246	275	lantern		RC 344	A2 179	381		
RC 290	A3 245	274			RC 345	A2 177	379		
RC 291	A3 244	273			RC 346	A2 176	378		
RC 292	A3 243	272			RC 347	A2 175	377	lantern	
RC 293	A3 242	271			RC 348	A2 174	374		
RC 294	A3 241	270			RC 349	A2 173	376		
RC 295	A3 240	269	lantern		RC 350	A2 172	375		
RC 296	A3 239	268			RC 351	A2 171	373		
RC 297	A3 238	267			RC 352	A2 170	372	lantern	
RC 298	A3 237	266			RC 353	A2 169	371		
RC 299	A3 235	265	lantern		RC 354	A2 168	370		
RC 300	A3 234	264			RC 355	A2 166	369		
RC 301	A3 233	263			RC 356	A2 165	368		
RC 302	A3 232	262			RC 357	A2 167	367	lantern	
RC 303	A3 230	260			RC 358	A2 164	365		
RC 304	A3 230	261	lantern	Duplicate No. A3 230	RC 359	A2 162	364		
RC 305	A3 228	259	lantern		RC 360	A2 162	363	lantern	Duplicate No. A2 162
RC 306	A3 227	258			RC 361	A2 160	362	lantern	
RC 307	A3 226	257			RC 362	A2 157	361	lantern	
RC 308	A3 225	256			RC 363	A2 148	357		
RC 309	A3 224	255			RC 364	A2 152	360	lantern	
RC 310	A3 223	254			RC 365	A2 151	359	lantern	
RC 311	A3 222	253	lantern		RC 366	A2 147	356		
RC 312	A3 220	252	lantern	Duplicate No. A3 220	RC 367	A2 146	355		
RC 313	A3 220	251			RC 368	A2 145	354		
RC 314	A3 219	250			RC 369	A2 178	380		
RC 315	A3 218	249			RC 370	A2 143	353		
RC 316	A3 217	248			RC 371	A2 142	352	lantern	
RC 317	A3 216	247			RC 372	A2 149	358	lantern	
RC 318	A3 215	246			RC 373	A2 120	340		
RC 319	A3 214	245	lantern		RC 374	A2 127	337		
RC 320	A3 213	244			RC 375	A2 139	349		
RC 321	A3 212	243			RC 376	A2 140	350	lantern	

RC number[1]	Packet number[2]	Ink number[3]	Slide size[4]	Comments[5]	RC number[1]	Packet number[2]	Ink number[3]	Slide size[4]	Comments[5]
RC 377	A2 138	348	lantern		RC 432	A1 71	459		
RC 378	A2 136	347			RC 433	A1 70	458		
RC 379	A2 135	346			RC 434	A1 66	454		
RC 380	A2 134	345			RC 435	A1 68	456		
RC 381	A2 133	344			RC 436	A1 69	457	lantern	
RC 382	A2 131	342			RC 437	A1 67	455		
RC 383	A2 130	341	lantern		RC 438	A1 54	441		
RC 384	A2 132	343	lantern		RC 439	A1 55	443		
RC 385	A2 129	340			RC 440	A1 66	445		
RC 386	A2 128	339			RC 441	A1 52	439		
RC 387	A2 127	338	lantern	Duplicate No. A2 127	RC 442	A1 46	433	lantern	
RC 388	A2 116	337	lantern		RC 443	A1 60	450	lantern	Duplicate No. A1 60
RC 389	A2 126	336			RC 444	A1 59	448		
RC 390	A2 124	344			RC 445	A1 58	447		
RC 391	A2 123	343			RC 446	A1 57	446		
RC 392	A2 125	335	lantern		RC 447	A1 56	444	lantern	
RC 393	A2 122	342	lantern		RC 448	A1 54	442	lantern	Duplicate No. A1 54
RC 394	A2 121	341			RC 449	A1 53	440		
RC 395	A2 120	339	lantern	Duplicate No. A2 120	RC 450	A1 51	438		
RC 396	A2 118	338	lantern		RC 451	A1 62	452		
RC 397	A2 111	336			RC 452	A1 50	436		
RC 398	A2 110	335			RC 453	A1 50	437	lantern	Duplicate No. A1 50
RC 399	A2 141	351			RC 454	A1 49	435		
RC 400	A2 109	334	lantern		RC 455	A1 48	434		
RC 401	A1 86	475			RC 456	A1 37	425		
RC 402	A2 107	333			RC 457	A1 85	474	lantern	
RC 403	A2 106	332			RC 458	A1 35	422		
RC 404	A2 105	331			RC 459	A1 10	403		
RC 405	A2 104	330			RC 460	A1 43	431		
RC 406	A2 103	329			RC 461	A1 42	430		
RC 407	A2 102	328	lantern		RC 462	A1 41	429		
RC 408	A2 101	327			RC 463	A1 40	428	lantern	
RC 409	A1 99	482			RC 464	A1 38	426		
RC 410	A1 98	481	lantern		RC 465	A1 39	427		
RC 411	A1 95	480	lantern		RC 466	A1 44	432		
RC 412	A1 93	479	lantern		RC 467	A1 36	424		
RC 413	A1 91	478			RC 468	A1 35	423	lantern	Duplicate No. A1 35
RC 414	A1 74	461			RC 469	A1 34	421		
RC 415	A1 90	477	lantern	Duplicate No. A1 90	RC 470	A1 29	417		
RC 416	A1 90	476			RC 471	A1 12	405		
RC 417	A1 61	451	lantern		RC 472	A1 31	419		
RC 418	A1 75	462			RC 473	A1 30	418	lantern	
RC 419	A1 84	473			RC 474	A1 33	420		
RC 420	A1 83	472			RC 475	A1 28	416		
RC 421	A1 82	471			RC 476	A1 27	415		
RC 422	A1 81	470			RC 477	A1 24	414	lantern	
RC 423	A1 80	469			RC 478	A1 26	413		
RC 424	A1 79	468	lantern		RC 479	A1 25	412		
RC 425	A1 78	467			RC 480	A1 22	411		
RC 426	A1 77	466			RC 481	A1 21	410		
RC 427	A1 76	464			RC 482	A1 20	409	lantern	
RC 428	A1 75	463	lantern	Duplicate No. A1 75	RC 483	A1 19	408	lantern	Duplicate No. A1 19
RC 429	A1 60	449			RC 484	A1 76	465	lantern	
RC 430	A1 63	453			RC 485	A1 19	407		
RC 431	A1 72	460			RC 486	A1 18	406		

RC number[1]	Packet number[2]	Ink number[3]	Slide size[4]	Comments[5]	RC number[1]	Packet number[2]	Ink number[3]	Slide size[4]	Comments[5]
RC 487	A1 10	404	lantern	Duplicate No. A1 10	RC 542	B6 501	855	lantern	
RC 488	A1 8	402			RC 543	B6 500	854	lantern	
RC 489	A1 5	401			RC 544	B5 499	853		
RC 490	A1 4	400			RC 545	B5 498	852		
RC 491	A1 1	399			RC 546	B5 497	851		
RC 492	B6 554	905	lantern		RC 547	B5 495	849		
RC 493	B6 549	904			RC 548	B5 494	848		
RC 494	B6 550	903			RC 549	B5 493	847		
RC 495	B6 548	902			RC 550	B5 492	846	lantern	
RC 496	B6 547	901			RC 551	B5 491	845		
RC 497	B6 545	899	lantern		RC 552	B5 490	844		
RC 498	B6 546	900			RC 553	B5 489	843		
RC 499	B6 544	898			RC 554	B5 488	842		
RC 500	B6 543	897			RC 555	B5 487	841		
RC 501	B6 542	896			RC 556	B5 486	840		
RC 502	B6 541	895			RC 557	B5 485	839		
RC 503	B6 540	894			RC 558	B5 484	838		
RC 504	B6 539	893			RC 559	B5 483	837		
RC 505	B6 538	892			RC 560	B5 482	836	lantern	
RC 506	B6 537	891	lantern		RC 561	B5 481	835	lantern	
RC 507	B6 536	890	lantern		RC 562	B5 480	834		
RC 508	B6 535	889			RC 563	B5 479	832		
RC 509	B6 534	888			RC 564	B5 478	833		
RC 510	B6 533	887			RC 565	B5 461	817		
RC 511	B6 532	886			RC 566	B5 476	831		
RC 512	B6 531	885			RC 567	B5 475	830		
RC 513	B6 530	884			RC 568	B5 474	829		
RC 514	B6 529	883			RC 569	B5 473	828		
RC 515	B6 528	882			RC 570	B5 472	827	lantern	
RC 516	B6 527	881			RC 571	B5 471	826		
RC 517	B6 526	880			RC 572	B5 470	825		
RC 518	B6 525	879	lantern		RC 573	B5 468	824		
RC 519	B6 524	878			RC 574	B5 467	823		
RC 520	B6 523	877			RC 575	B5 466	822		
RC 521	B6 522	876			RC 576	B5 465	821		
RC 522	B6 521	875			RC 577	B5 464	820		
RC 523	B6 520	874			RC 578	B5 463	819		
RC 524	B6 519	873			RC 579	B5 462	818	lantern	
RC 525	B6 518	872			RC 580	B5 459	815		
RC 526	B6 504	858			RC 581	B5 460	816		
RC 527	B6 516	870			RC 582	B5 456	812		
RC 528	B6 515	869	lantern		RC 583	B5 458	814		
RC 529	B6 514	868			RC 584	B5 457	813		
RC 530	B6 513	867			RC 585	B5 456	811		
RC 531	B6 512	866			RC 586	B5 455	810		
RC 532	B6 511	865			RC 587	B5 454	809		
RC 533	B6 510	864			RC 588	B5 442	797		
RC 534	B6 509	863			RC 589	B5 452	808	lantern	
RC 535	B6 508	862	lantern		RC 590	B5 451	807		
RC 536	B6 503	857			RC 591	B5 450	806		
RC 537	B6 506	860			RC 592	B5 449	805		
RC 538	B6 505	859			RC 593	B5 448	804		
RC 539	B6 517	871			RC 594	B5 447	803		
RC 540	B6 507	861			RC 595	B5 446	802		
RC 541	B6 502	856			RC 596	B5 445	801		

RC number[1]	Packet number[2]	Ink number[3]	Slide size[4]	Comments[5]	RC number[1]	Packet number[2]	Ink number[3]	Slide size[4]	Comments[5]
RC 597	B5 444	800			RC 652	B4 387	745		
RC 598	B5 443	799			RC 653	B4 386	744	lantern	
RC 599	B5 442	798	lantern	Duplicate No. B5 442	RC 654	B4 385	743		
RC 600	B5 441	796			RC 655	B4 384	742		
RC 601	B5 440	795			RC 656	B4 383	741		
RC 602	B5 439	794			RC 657	B4 382	740		
RC 603	B5 438	793			RC 658	B4 381	739		
RC 604	B5 437	792			RC 659	B4 380	738		
RC 605	B5 436	791			RC 660	B4 379	737		
RC 606	B5 435	790			RC 661	B4 378	736		
RC 607	B5 434	789			RC 662	B4 377	735		
RC 608	B5 433	788			RC 663	B4 376	734		
RC 609	B5 432	787	lantern		RC 664	B4 375	733	lantern	
RC 610	B5 431	786			RC 665	B4 374	732		
RC 611	B5 430	785			RC 666	B4 373	731		
RC 612	B5 429	784			RC 667	B4 372	730		
RC 613	B5 428	783			RC 668	B4 371	729		
RC 614	B5 427	782			RC 669	B4 370	728		
RC 615	B5 426	781			RC 670	B4 369	727		
RC 616	B5 425	780			RC 671	B4 368	726		
RC 617	B5 424	779			RC 672	B4 367	725		
RC 618	B5 423	778			RC 673	B4 366	724		
RC 619	B5 422	777	lantern		RC 674	B4 365	723	lantern	
RC 620	B5 421	776			RC 675	B4 364	722		
RC 621	B5 420	775			RC 676	B4 363	721		
RC 622	B5 419	774			RC 677	B4 362	720		
RC 623	B5 417	773			RC 678	B4 361	719		
RC 624	B5 416	772			RC 679	B4 360	718		
RC 625	B5 415	771			RC 680	B4 351	708		
RC 626	B5 414	770			RC 681	B4 358	716		
RC 627	B5 413	769			RC 682	B4 357	715		
RC 628	B5 412	768	lantern		RC 683	B4 356	714		
RC 629	B5 410	767			RC 684	B4 355	712	lantern	Duplicate No. B4 355
RC 630	B5 409	766			RC 685	B4 354	711		
RC 631	B5 408	765			RC 686	B4 353	710		
RC 632	B5 407	764			RC 687	B4 352	709		
RC 633	B5 406	763			RC 688	B4 355	713		
RC 634	B5 405	762			RC 689	B4 350	707		
RC 635	B5 404	761			RC 690	B4 349	706		
RC 636	B5 403	760			RC 691	B4 347	705		
RC 637	B5 402	759			RC 692	B4 346	704		
RC 638	B5 401	758			RC 693	B4 345	703	lantern	
RC 639	B5 400	757	lantern		RC 694	B4 344	703		
RC 640	B4 399	756	lantern		RC 695	B4 342	701		
RC 641	B4 398	755			RC 696	B4 343	702		
RC 642	B4 397	754			RC 697	B4 341	700		
RC 643	B4 396	753			RC 698	B4 340	699		
RC 644	B4 395	752			RC 699	B4 339	698		
RC 645	B4 392	749			RC 700	B4 338	697		
RC 646	B4 393	750			RC 701	B4 337	696		
RC 647	B4 394	751			RC 702	B4 336	695		
RC 648	B4 359	717			RC 703	B4 335	694	lantern	
RC 649	B4 390	748			RC 704	B4 334	693		
RC 650	B4 389	747			RC 705	B4 333	692		
RC 651	B4 388	746			RC 706	B4 332	691		

RC number[1]	Packet number[2]	Ink number[3]	Slide size[4]	Comments[5]	RC number[1]	Packet number[2]	Ink number[3]	Slide size[4]	Comments[5]
RC 707	B4 331	690			RC 762	section presumed lost during processing			
RC 708	B4 330	689			RC 763	section presumed lost during processing			
RC 709	B4 329	688			RC 764	section presumed lost during processing			
RC 700	B4 328	687			RC 765	section presumed lost during processing			
RC 711	B4 327	686			RC 766	section presumed lost during processing			
RC 712	B4 326	685			RC 767	section presumed lost during processing			
RC 713	B4 324	682			RC 768	section presumed lost during processing			
RC 714	B4 325	684			RC 769	section presumed lost during processing			
RC 715	B4 323	681			RC 770	section presumed lost during processing			
RC 716	B4 322	680			RC 771	B3 270	662	lantern	
RC 717	B4 321	679			RC 772	section presumed lost during processing			
RC 718	B4 320	678			RC 773	section presumed lost during processing			
RC 719	B4 319	677			RC 774	section presumed lost during processing			
RC 720	B4 318	676			RC 775	section presumed lost during processing			
RC 721	B4 317	675			RC 776	section presumed lost during processing			
RC 722	B4 316	674			RC 777	section presumed lost during processing			
RC 723	B4 315	673			RC 778	section presumed lost during processing			
RC 724	B4 314	672			RC 779	section presumed lost during processing			
RC 725	B4 313	671			RC 780	section presumed lost during processing			
RC 726	B4 310	668			RC 781	B3 260	661	lantern	
RC 727	B4 312	670			RC 782	section presumed lost during processing			
RC 728	B4 311	669	lantern		RC 783	section presumed lost during processing			
RC 729	B4 325	683	lantern	Duplicate No. B4 325	RC 784	section presumed lost during processing			
RC 730	B4 303	667	lantern		RC 785	section presumed lost during processing			
RC 731	B3 ?	666			RC 786	section presumed lost during processing			
RC 732	section presumed lost during processing				RC 787	section presumed lost during processing			
RC 733	section presumed lost during processing				RC 788	section presumed lost during processing			
RC 734	section presumed lost during processing				RC 789	section presumed lost during processing			
RC 735	section presumed lost during processing				RC 790	section presumed lost during processing			
RC 736	section presumed lost during processing				RC 791	B3 240	660	lantern	
RC 737	section presumed lost during processing				RC 792	section presumed lost during processing			
RC 738	section presumed lost during processing				RC 793	section presumed lost during processing			
RC 739	section presumed lost during processing				RC 794	section presumed lost during processing			
RC 740	section presumed lost during processing				RC 795	section presumed lost during processing			
RC 741	B3 298	665	lantern		RC 796	section presumed lost during processing			
RC 742	section presumed lost during processing				RC 797	section presumed lost during processing			
RC 743	section presumed lost during processing				RC 798	section presumed lost during processing			
RC 744	section presumed lost during processing				RC 799	section presumed lost during processing			
RC 745	section presumed lost during processing				RC 800	B3 250	659	lantern	
RC 746	section presumed lost during processing				RC 801	section presumed lost during processing			
RC 747	section presumed lost during processing				RC 802	section presumed lost during processing			
RC 748	section presumed lost during processing				RC 803	section presumed lost during processing			
RC 749	section presumed lost during processing				RC 804	section presumed lost during processing			
RC 750	section presumed lost during processing				RC 805	section presumed lost during processing			
RC 751	B3 289	664	lantern		RC 806	section presumed lost during processing			
RC 752	section presumed lost during processing				RC 807	section presumed lost during processing			
RC 753	section presumed lost during processing				RC 808	section presumed lost during processing			
RC 754	section presumed lost during processing				RC 809	section presumed lost during processing			
RC 755	section presumed lost during processing				RC 810	B3 230	658	lantern	
RC 756	section presumed lost during processing				RC 811	section presumed lost during processing			
RC 757	section presumed lost during processing				RC 812	section presumed lost during processing			
RC 758	section presumed lost during processing				RC 813	section presumed lost during processing			
RC 759	section presumed lost during processing				RC 814	section presumed lost during processing			
RC 760	section presumed lost during processing				RC 815	section presumed lost during processing			
RC 761	B3 280	663	lantern		RC 816	section presumed lost during processing			

RC number[1]	Packet number[2]	Ink number[3]	Slide size[4]	Comments[5]	RC number[1]	Packet number[2]	Ink number[3]	Slide size[4]	Comments[5]
RC 817	section presumed lost during processing				RC 872	B2 145	599	lantern	
RC 818	section presumed lost during processing				RC 873	B2 168	622		
RC 819	section presumed lost during processing				RC 874	B2 167	621		
RC 820	B3 220	657	lantern		RC 875	B2 166	620		
RC 821	section presumed lost during processing				RC 876	B2 165	619		
RC 822	section presumed lost during processing				RC 877	B2 164	618		
RC 823	section presumed lost during processing				RC 878	B2 163	617		
RC 824	section presumed lost during processing				RC 879	B2 162	616		
RC 825	section presumed lost during processing				RC 880	B2 160	614		
RC 826	section presumed lost during processing				RC 881	B2 161	615		
RC 827	section presumed lost during processing				RC 882	B2 159	613		
RC 828	section presumed lost during processing				RC 883	B2 158	612		
RC 829	section presumed lost during processing				RC 884	B2 157	611		
RC 830	B3 201	656	lantern		RC 885	B2 156	609	lantern	Duplicate No. B2 156
RC 831	section presumed lost during processing				RC 886	B2 155	608	lantern	
RC 832	section presumed lost during processing				RC 887	B2 154	607		
RC 833	section presumed lost during processing				RC 888	B2 153	606		
RC 834	section presumed lost during processing				RC 889	B2 156	610		
RC 835	section presumed lost during processing				RC 890	B2 151	605		
RC 836	section presumed lost during processing				RC 891	B2 150	604		
RC 837	section presumed lost during processing				RC 892	B2 149	603		
RC 838	section presumed lost during processing				RC 893	B2 148	602		
RC 839	section presumed lost during processing				RC 894	B2 147	601		
RC 840	B3 210	655	lantern		RC 895	B2 146	600		
RC 841	B2 200	654			RC 896	B2 135	589	lantern	
RC 842	B2 198	652	lantern	Duplicate No. B2 198	RC 897	B2 144	598		
RC 843	B2 189	641			RC 898	B2 143	597		
RC 844	B2 197	650			RC 899	B2 142	596		
RC 845	B2 196	649			RC 900	B2 141	595		
RC 846	B2 195	648			RC 901	B2 140	594		
RC 847	B2 194	647			RC 902	B2 139	593		
RC 848	B2 193	646			RC 903	B2 138	592		
RC 849	B2 191	644			RC 904	B2 137	591		
RC 850	B2 198	651			RC 905	B2 136	590		
RC 851	B2 190	643			RC 906	B2 120	583	lantern	
RC 852	B2 189	642	lantern	Duplicate No. B2 189	RC 907	B2 134	588		
RC 853	B2 186	638			RC 908	B2 133	587		
RC 854	B2 187	639			RC 909	B2 132	586		
RC 855	B2 188	640			RC 910	B2 131	585		
RC 856	B2 185	637			RC 911	B2 130	584		
RC 857	B2 184	636			RC 912	B1 29	509		
RC 858	B2 183	635			RC 913	B1 28	508		
RC 859	B2 192	645			RC 914	B1 27	507		
RC 860	B2 180	634			RC 915	B1 26	506		
RC 861	B2 170	624			RC 916	B1 25	505		
RC 862	B2 179	633			RC 917	B1 24	504		
RC 863	B2 178	632	lantern		RC 918	B1 23	503		
RC 864	B2 177	631			RC 919	B1 22	502		
RC 865	B2 176	630			RC 920	B1 21	501		
RC 866	B2 175	629			RC 921	B1 199	953		
RC 867	B2 174	628			RC 922	B1 18	498		
RC 868	B2 173	627			RC 923	B1 17	497		
RC 869	B2 172	626			RC 924	B1 16	496		
RC 870	B2 171	625			RC 925	B1 15	495		
RC 871	B2 169	623			RC 926	B1 14	494		

Appendix

RC number[1]	Packet number[2]	Ink number[3]	Slide size[4]	Comments[5]	RC number[1]	Packet number[2]	Ink number[3]	Slide size[4]	Comments[5]
RC 927	B1 13	493			RC 971	B1 67	549		
RC 928	B1 12	492			RC 972	B1 66	548		
RC 929	B2 110	581			RC 973	B1 65	547		
RC 930	B2 110	582	lantern	Duplicate No. B2 110	RC 974	B1 64	546		
RC 931	B1 09	488			RC 975	B1 63	544		
RC 932	B1 08	487			RC 976	B1 62	543		
RC 933	B1 07	486			RC 977	B1 61	542		
RC 934	B1 06	485			RC 978	B1 50	532		
RC 935	B2 105	580			RC 979	B1 59	541		
RC 936	B1 04	484			RC 980	B1 57	539	lantern	
RC 937	B1 03	483			RC 981	B1 56	538		
RC 938	B2 102	579			RC 982	B1 58	540		
RC 939	B2 101	578			RC 983	B1 55	537		
RC 940	B2 100	577	lantern		RC 984	B1 54	536		
RC 941	B1 97	576			RC 985	B1 53	535		
RC 942	B1 95	574			RC 986	B1 52	534		
RC 943	B1 96	575			RC 987	B1 49	531		
RC 944	B1 94	573			RC 988	B1 51	533		
RC 945	B1 93	572			RC 989	B1 48	529	lantern	Duplicate No. B1 48
RC 946	B1 92	571			RC 990	B1 48	530		
RC 947	B1 19	499			RC 991	B1 47	528		
RC 948	B1 90	570	lantern		RC 992	B1 46	527		
RC 949	B1 89	569			RC 993	B1 45	526		
RC 950	B1 76	558			RC 994	B1 44	525		
RC 951	B1 87	568	lantern		RC 995	B1 43	524		
RC 952	B1 84	565			RC 996	B1 42	523		
RC 953	B1 85	566			RC 997	B1 41	522		
RC 954	B1 86	567			RC 998	B1 40	521		
RC 955	B1 83	564			RC 999	B1 39	520	lantern	
RC 956	B1 82	565			RC 1000	B1 38	519		
RC 957	B1 81	564			RC 1001	B1 37	518		
RC 958	B1 79	561			RC 1002	B1 36	517		
RC 959	B1 80	562	lantern	Duplicate No. B1 80	RC 1003	B1 35	516		
RC 960	B1 77	559			RC 1004	B1 34	515		
RC 961	B1 80	563			RC 1005	B1 33	514		
RC 962	B1 78	560			RC 1006	B1 31	512		
RC 963	B1 75	557			RC 1007	B1 30	511	lantern	Duplicate No. B1 30
RC 964	B1 74	556			RC 1008	B1 30	510		
RC 965	B1 73	555			RC 1009	B1 20	500		
RC 966	B1 72	554			RC 1010	B1 32	513		
RC 967	B1 71	553			RC 1011	B1 10	490		
RC 968	B1 70	552			RC 1012	B1 11	491		
RC 969	B1 69	551	lantern		RC 1013	B1 10	489		Duplicate No. B1 10
RC 970	B1 68	550							

References

Allis, E.P. (1889) The anatomy and development of the lateral line system in *Amia calva*. J. Morphol., *2:* 463–540.

Allis, E.P. (1897) The cranial muscles and cranial and first spinal nerves in *Amia calva*. J. Morphol., *12:* 487–808.

Allis, E.P. (1920) The branches of the branchial nerves of fishes, with special reference to *Polyodon spathula*. J. Comp. Neurol., *32:* 137–154.

Allis, E.P. (1922) The cranial anatomy of *Polypterus*, with special reference to *Polypterus bichir*. J. Anat., *56:* 189–294.

Anthony, J. (1980) Évocation de travaux français sur *Latimeria* notamment depuis 1972. Proc. R. Soc., Ser. B., *208:* 349–367.

Atz, J.W. (1976) *Latimeria* babies are born, not hatched. Underwater Naturalist, *9:* 4–7.

Bartheld, C.S. von, H.W. Lindörfer, and D.L. Meyer (1987) The nervus terminalis also exists in cyclostomes and birds. Cell Tissue Res., *250:* 431–434.

Bemis, W.E., and T.E. Hetherington (1982) The rostral organ of *Latimeria chalumnae:* morphological evidence of an electroreceptive function. Copeia, *1982:* 467–471.

Bemis, W.E., W.W. Burggren, and N.E. Kemp (eds.) (1987) The Biology and Evolution of Lungfishes. Alan R. Liss, New York.

Bemis, W.E., and R.G. Northcutt (1991) Innervation of the basicranial muscle of *Latimeria chalumnae*. Env. Biol. Fishes, *32:* 147–158.

Bemis, W.E., and L. Grande (1992) Early development of the actinopterygian head. 1. External development and staging of the paddlefish *Polydon spathula*. J. Morphol., *213:* 47–83.

Bertmar, G. (1965) The olfactory organ and upper lips in Dipnoi, an embryological study. Acta Zool., *46:* 1–40.

Bjerring, H.C. (1972) The *nervus rarus* in coelacanthiform phylogeny. Zool. Scripta, *1:* 57–68.

Bjerring, H.C. (1973) Relationships of coelacanthiforms. *In* Interrelationships of Fishes (ed. by P.H. Greenwood, R.S. Miles, and C. Patterson), Linnean Society of London, Academic Press, London, pp. 179–205.

Bjerring, H.C. (1977) A contribution to structural analysis of the head of craniate animals. The orbit and its contents in 20–22 mm embryos of the North American actinopterygian *Amia calva* L., with particular reference to the evolutionary significance of an aberrant, nonocular, orbital muscle innervated by the oculomotor nerve and notes on the metameric character of the head in craniates. Zool. Scripta, *6:* 127–183.

Bodznick, D.A., and R.G. Northcutt (1980) Segregation of electro- and mechanical inputs to the elasmobranch medulla. Brain Res., *195:* 313–321.

Board, R.L., and C.B.G. Campbell (1977) Structural and functional organization of the lateral line system of sharks. Amer. Zool., *17:* 431–441.

Board, R.L., and D.G. Sperry (1991) Topography and nerve supply of the cucullaris (Trapezius) of skates. J. Morphol., *207:* 165–172.

Bruton, M.N., and S.E. Coutouvidis (1991) An inventory of all known specimens of the coelacanth *Latimeria chalumnae*, with comments on trends in the catches. Env. Biol. Fishes, *33:* 371–390.

Bullock, T.H., and W. Heiligenberg (eds.) (1986) Electroreception. Wiley, New York.

Butler, A.B., and R.G. Northcutt (1992) Retinal projections in the bowfin, *Amia calva:* cytoarchitectonic and experimental analysis. Brain, Behav. Evol., *39:* 169–194.

Cloutier, R. (1991) Patterns, trends, and rates of evolution within the Actinistia. Env. Biol. Fishes, *32:* 23–58.

Coghill, G.E. (1902) The cranial nerves of *Amblystoma tigrinum*. J. Comp. Neurol., *12:* 205–289.

Coghill, G.E. (1916) Correlated anatomical and physiological studies of the growth of the nervous system of Amphibia. J. Comp. Neurol., *26:* 247–340.

Cole, F.J. (1896) On the cranial nerves of *Chimaera monstrosa* (Linn. 1754); with a discussion of the lateral line system, and of the morphology of the chorda tympani. Trans. R. Soc. Edinb., *38:* 631–680, 2 pl.

Cole, F.J., and W.J. Dakin (1906) Further observations on the cranial nerves of *Chimaera*. Anat. Anz., *28:* 595–599.

Compagno, L.J.V. (1979) Coelacanths: shark relatives or bony fishes? Occ. Pap. Calif. Acad. Sci., no. *134:* 45–52.

Coombs, S., P. Görner, and P. Münz (eds.) (1989) Neurobiology and Evolution of the Lateral Line System. Springer-Verlag, New York.

Damas, H. (1951) Observations sur le développment des ganglions crâniens chez *Lampetra fluviatilis* (L.). Arch. de Biol., *62:* 65–95.

Derivot, J.H. (1984) Functional anatomy of the peripheral olfactory system of the African lungfish *Protopterus annectens* Owen: macroscopic, microscopic, and morphometric aspects. Amer. J. Anat., *169:* 177–192.

Duellman, W.E., and L. Trueb (1986) Biology of Amphibians. McGraw Hill, New York.

El-Toubi, M.R., and I. Abdel-Aziz (1956) On the chondocranium and cranial nerves of larval *Polypterus*. Bull. Fac. Sci., No. *33:* Cairo University Press, pp. 1–44.

Finger, T. (1983) The gustatory system in teleost fish. *In* Fish Neurobiology (ed. by R.G. Northcutt, and R.E. Davis), University of Michigan Press, New York, pp. 285–309.

Forey, P.L. (1987) Relationships of lungfishes. *In* Biology and Evolution of Lungfishes (ed. by W.E. Bemis, W.W. Burggren, and N.E. Kemp), Alan R. Liss, New York, pp. 75–91.

Forey, P.L. (1991) *Latimeria chalumnae* and its pedigree. *In* The Biology of *Latimeria chalumnae* and Evolution of Coelacanths (ed. by J.A. Musick, M.N. Bruton, and E.K. Balon), Kluwer, Dordrecht, pp. 75–97.

Fox, H. (1965) Early development of the head and pharynx of *Neoceratodus* with a consideration of its phylogeny. J. Zool., *146:* 470–554.

Freihofer, W.C. (1978) Cranial nerves of a percoid fish, *Polycentrus schomburgkii* (Family Nandidae), a contribution to the morphology and classification of the order Perciformes. Occas. Pap. Cal. Acad. Sci., No. *128:* 78 pages.

Fricke, H., O. Reinicke, H. Hofer, and W. Nachtigall (1987) Locomotion of the coelacanth *Latimeria chalumnae* in its natural environment. Nature, *329:* 331–333.

Fritzsch, B. (1987) Inner ear of the coelacanth fish *Latimeria* has tetrapod affinities. Nature, *327:* 153–154.

Fritzsch, B. (1992) The water-to-land transition: evolution of the tetrapod basilar papilla, middle ear, and auditory nuclei. *In* The Evolutionary Biology of Hearing (ed. by D.B. Webster, R.R. Fay, and A.N. Popper), Springer-Verlag, New York, pp. 351–375.

Fritzsch, B., and D. Bolz (1986) On the development of electroreceptive ampullary organs in *Triturus alpestris* (Amphibia: Urodela). Amphibia Reptilia, 7: 1–9.

Fritzsch, B., R. Sonntag, R. Dubuc, Y. Ohta, and S. Grillner (1990) Organization of the six motor nuclei innervating the ocular muscles in lamprey. J. Comp. Neurol., *294:* 491–506.

Grande, L., and W.E. Bemis (1991) Osteology and phylogenetic relationships of fossil and recent paddlefishes (Polyodontidae) with comments on the interrelationships of Acipenseriformes. J. Vert. Paleo. Spec. Memoir, *1:* 1–132.

Günther, C.A.L.G. (1872) An account of a ganoid fish from Queensland *(Ceratodus).* Pop. Sci. Rev. *11:* 257–266.

Hardisty, M.W. (1982) Lampreys and hagfishes: Analysis of cyclostome relationships. *In* The Biology of Lampreys, 4B (ed. by M.W. Hardisty, and I.C. Potter), Academic Press, New York, pp. 165–259.

Hensel, K. (1986) Morphologie et interprétation des canaux et canalicules sensoriels céphaliques de *Latimeria chalumnae* Smith, 1939 (Osteichthyes, Crossopterygii, Coelacanthiformes). Bull. Mus. Natl. Hist. Nat. Paris IV sér., *8:* 379–407.

Herrick, C.J. (1899) The cranial and first spinal nerves of *Menidia:* a contribution upon the nerve components of the bony fishes. J. Comp. Neurol., 9: 153–455.

Herrick, C.J. (1900) A contribution upon the cranial nerves of the codfish. J. Comp. Neurol., *10:* 265–316.

Herrick, C.J. (1901) The cranial nerves and cutaneous sense organs of the North American siluroid fishes. J. Comp. Neurol., *11:* 177–249.

Herrick, C.J. (1944) The cranial nerves. A review of fifty years. Denison University J. Sci. Lab. *38:* 41–51.

Hetherington, T.E., and W.E. Bemis (1979) Morphological evidence of an electroreceptive function of the rostral organ of *Latimeria chalumnae.* Amer. Zool. 19: 986 (Abstract).

Holmgren, N., and C.J. van der Horst (1925) Contribution to the morphology of the brain of *Ceratodus.* Acta Zool., 6: 59–165.

Jarvik, E. (1980) Basic Structure and Evolution of Vertebrates. 2 Vol. Academic Press, London.

Johnston, J.B. (1905) The cranial nerve components of *Petromyzon.* Gegenbaurs morph. Jb., *34:* 149–203.

Johnston, J.B. (1908a) Additional notes on the cranial nerves of Petromyzonts. J. Comp. Neurol., *18:* 569–608.

Johnston, J.B. (1908b) A note on the presence or absence of the glossopharyngeal nerve in myxinoids. Anat. Rec., *2:* 233–239.

Jollie, M. (1962) Chordate Morphology. Rheinhold, New York.

Jørgenson, J.M. (1991) Ciliated sensory cells in the rostral organ of the coelacanth *Latimeria chalumnae* (Smith 1939). Acta Zool., *72:* 121–124.

Kleerekoper, H. (1969) Olfaction in Fishes. Indiana University Press, Bloomington.

Kremers, J.-W.P.M., and R. Nieuwenhuys (1979) Topological analysis of the brain stem of the crossopterygian fish *Latimeria chalumnae.* J. Comp. Neurol., *187:* 613–638.

Kuppfer, C.W. von (1895) Über die Entwickelung des Kiemenskelets von Ammocoetes und die Organogene Bestimmung des Exoderms. Verh. Anat. Ges., Anat. Anz., *11:* 105–122.

Lagios, M.D. (1979) The coelacanth and the Chondrichthyes as sister groups: a review of shared apomorph characters and a cladistic analysis and reinterpretation. Occ. Pap. Calif. Acad. Sci., No. *134:* 25–44.

Landacre, F.L. (1910) The origin of the cranial ganglia in *Amerius.* J. Comp. Neurol., *20:* 309–411.

Landacre, F.L. (1912) The epibranchial placodes of *Lepidosteus osseus* and their relationship to the cerebral ganglia. J. Comp. Neurol., *22:* 1–69.

Landacre, F.L. (1916) The cerebral ganglia and early nerves of *Squalus acanthias.* J. Comp. Neurol., *27:* 20–55.

Landacre, F.L., and A.C. Conger (1913) The origin of the lateral line primordia in *Lepidosteus osseus.* J. Comp. Neurol., *23:* 575–633.

Langille, R.M., and B.K. Hall (1988) Role of the neural crest in development of the trabeculae and branchial arches in embryonic sea lamprey, *Petromyzon marinus* (L.). Development, *102:* 301–310.

Lauder, G.V., and K.F. Liem (1983) The evolution and interrelationships of the actinopterygian fishes. Bull. Mus. Comp. Zool., *150:* 95–197.

Lemire, M. (1971) Étude architectonique du rhombencéphale de *Latimeria chalumnae* Smith. Bull. Mus. Natn. Hist. Nat., Zoologie, *3:* 41–95.

Lindström, T. (1949) On the cranial nerves of the cyclostomes with special reference to *N. trigeminus.* Acta Zool. Stockh., *30:* 315–348.

McCready, P.J., and R.L. Boord (1976) The topography of the superficial roots and ganglia of the anterior lateral line nerve of the smooth dogfish, *Mustelus canis.* J. Morphol. *150:* 527–538.

Maddison, W.P., and D.R. Maddison (1992) MacClade: Analysis of Phylogeny and Character Evolution. Version 3.0s. Sinauer Associates Inc., Sunderland, MA.

Maisey, J.G. (1986) Heads and tails: A chordate phylogeny. Cladistics, *2:* 201–256.

Marinelli, W., and A. Strenger (1954) Vergleichende Anatomie und Morphologie der Wirbeltiere, *1:* 1–80.

Millot, J., and J. Anthony (1958) Anatomie de *Latimeria chalumnae.* I. Squelette, muscles et formations de soutien. Centre National de la Recherche Scientifique, Paris.

Millot, J., and J. Anthony (1965) Anatomie de *Latimeria chalumnae.* II. Système nerveux et organes des sens. Centre National de la Recherche Scientifique, Paris.

Millot, J., J. Anthony, and D. Robineau (1978) Anatomie de *Latimeria chalumnae.* III. Centre National de la Recherche Scientifique, Paris.

Musick, J.A., M.N. Bruton, and E.K. Balon (eds.) (1991) The Biology of *Latimeria chalumnae* and Evolution of Coelacanths. Kluwer, Dordrecht.

Myking, L.M. (1977) Old Four Legs: The living fossil. Sea Frontiers, *23:* 334–341.

Noden, D.M. (1991) Vertebrate craniofacial development: The relation between ontogenetic process and morphological outcome. Brain, Behav. Evol., *38:* 190–225.

Norris, H.W. (1924) Branchial nerve homologies. Zeitschr. f. Morph. u. Anthro. 24: 211–226.

Norris, H.W. (1925) Observations upon the peripheral distribution of the cranial nerves of certain ganoid fishes *(Amia, Lepidosteus, Polyodon, Scaphirhynchus* and *Acipenser).* J. Comp. Neurol., *39:* 345–432.

Norris, H.W., and S.P. Hughes (1920) The cranial, occipital, and anterior spinal nerves of the dogfish, *Squalus acanthias.* J. Comp. Neurol., *31:* 292–402.

Northcutt, R.G. (1978) Brain organization in the cartilaginous fishes. *In* Sensory Biology of Sharks, Skates and Rays (ed. by E.S. Hodgson, and R.F. Mathewson), Office of Naval Research, pp. 117–193.

Northcutt, R.G. (1980) Anatomical evidence of electroreception in the coelacanth *(Latimeria chalumnae).* Zbl. Vet. Med. Reihe C, *9:* 289–295.

Northcutt, R.G. (1985) The brain and sense organs of the earliest vertebrates: reconstruction of a morphotype. *In* Evolutionary Biology of Primitive Fishes (ed. by R.E. Foreman, A. Grobman, J.M. Doff, and R. Olsson). Plenum, New York, pp. 81–112.

Northcutt, R.G. (1986) Embryonic origin of amphibian electroreceptors. Soc. Neurosci. Abstr., *12:* 103.

Northcutt, R.G. (1987) Lungfish neural characters and their bearing on Sarcopterygian phylogeny. *In* The Biology and Evolution of Lungfishes (ed. by W.E. Bemis, W.W. Burggren, and N.E. Kemp), Alan R. Liss, New York, pp. 277–297.

Northcutt, R.G. (1989) The phylogenetic distribution and innervation of craniate mechanoreceptive lateral lines. *In* The Mechanosensory Lateral Line: Neurobiology and Evolution (ed. by S. Coombs, P. Görner, and H. Munz), Springer-Verlag, New York, pp. 17–78.

Northcutt, R.G. (1990) Ontogeny and phylogeny: a re-evaluation of conceptual relationships and some applications. Brain, Behav. Evol., *36:* 116–140.

Northcutt, R.G. (1992a) The phylogeny of octavolateralis ontogenies: a reaffirmation of Garstang's phylogenetic hypothesis. *In* Evolutionary Biology of Hearing (ed. by A. Popper, D. Webster, and R. Fay), Springer, New York, pp. 21–47.

Northcutt, R.G. (1992b) Distribution and innervation of lateral line organs in the axolotl. J. Comp. Neurol., *325:* 95–123.

Northcutt, R.G., and R.L. Puzdrowski (1988) Projections of the olfactory bulb and nervus terminalis in the silver lamprey. Brain, Behav. Evol., *32:* 96–107.

Northcutt, R.G., and M.F. Wullimann (1988) The visual system in teleost fishes: morphological patterns and trends. *In* Sensory Biology of Aquatic Animals (ed. by J. Atema, R.R. Fay, A.N. Popper, and W.N. Tavolga), Springer, New York, pp. 515–552.

Northcutt, R.G., T.J. Neary, and D. Senn (1978) Observations on the brain of the coelacanth *Latimeria chalumnae:* External anatomy and quantitative analysis. J. Morphol., *155:* 181–192.

Northcutt, R.G., B. Fritzsch, and K. Brändle (1990) Experimental evidence that ampullary organs of salamanders derive from placodal material. Soc. Neurosci. Abstr., *16:* 129.

Patterson, C. (1982) Morphology and interrelationships of primitive actinopterygian fishes. Amer. Zool., *22:* 241–259.

Pehrson, T. (1949) The ontogeny of the lateral line system in the head of dipnoans. Acta Zool., *30:* 153–182.

Pinkus, E. (1895) Die Hirnnerven des *Protopterus annectens.* Morphol. Arb., *4:* 275–346.

Platt, J.B. (1896) Ontogenetic differentiations of the ectoderm in *Necturus.* J. Microsc. Sci., *38:* 485–547.

Popper, A., D. Webster, and R. Fay (eds.) (1992) Evolutionary Biology of Hearing. Springer, New York.

Romer, A.S. (1972) The Vertebrate Body. Saunders, Philadelphia.

Rosen, D.E., P.L. Forey, B.G. Gardiner, and C. Patterson (1981) Lungfishes, tetrapods, paleontology and plesiomorphy. Bull. Amer. Mus. Nat. Hist., *167:* 159–276.

Rüdebeck, B. (1944) Does an accessory olfactory bulb exist in Dipnoi? Acta Zool., *25:* 89–96.

Rüdebeck, B. (1945) Contribution to forebrain morphology in Dipnoi. Acta Zool., *26:* 10–156.

Sanders, A. (1889) Contributions to the anatomy of the central nervous system in *Ceratodus forsteri.* Ann. Mag. Nat. Hist. *3:* 157–188.

Schnitzlein, H.N., and E.C. Crosby (1967) The telencephalon of the lungfish *Protopterus.* J.F. Hirnforsch., *9:* 105–149.

Schultze, H.-P. (1991) A comparison of controversial hypotheses on the origin of tetrapods. *In* Origins of the Higher Groups of Tetrapods (ed. by H.-P. Schultze, and L. Trueb), Cornell University Press, Ithaca, pp. 29–67.

Smeets, W.J.A.J., R. Nieuwenhuys, and B.L. Roberts (1983) The Central Nervous System of Cartilaginous Fishes. Springer, New York.

Smith, C.L., C.S. Rand, B. Schaeffer, and J.W. Atz (1975) *Latimeria,* the living coelacanth, is ovoviviparous. Science, *190:* 1105–1106.

Smith, J.L.B. (1939a) A living fish of Mesozoic type. Nature, *143:* 455–456.

Smith, J.L.B. (1939b) A living coelacanthid fish from South Africa. Trans. Roy. Soc. South Africa, *28:* 1–106.

Smith, S.C., M.J. Lannoo, and J.B. Armstrong (1988) Lateral-line neuromast development in *Ambystoma mexicanum* and a comparison with *Rana pipiens.* J. Morphol., *198:* 367–379.

Sokol, O.M. (1975) The phylogeny of anuran larvae: a new look. Copeia, *1975:* 1–23.

Song, J., and R.G. Northcutt (1991a) Morphology, distribution and innervation of the lateral-line receptors of the Florida gar, *Lepisosteus platyrhincus.* Brain, Behav. Evol., *37:* 10–37.

Song, J., and R.G. Northcutt (1991b) The primary projections of the lateral-line nerves of the Florida gar, *Lepisosteus platyrhincus.* Brain, Behav. Evol., *37:* 38–63.

Stone, L.S. (1922) Experiments on the development of the cranial ganglia and the lateral line sense organs in *Ambystoma punctatum.* J. Exp. Zool., *35:* 421–495.

Strong, O.S. (1895) The cranial nerves of Amphibia. J. Morphol., *10:* 101–231.

Swofford, D.L. (1991) PAUP: Phylogenetic Analysis Using Parsimony. Version 3.0. Computer program distributed by the Illinois Natural History Survey, Champaign, IL.

Wicht, H., and R.G. Northcutt (1990) Retinofugal and retinopetal projections in the Pacific hagfish, *Eptatretus stouti.* Brain, Behav. Evol., *36:* 315–328.

Wiley, E.O. (1979) Ventral gill arch muscles and the phylogenetic relationships of *Latimeria. In* The Biology and Physiology of the Living Coelacanth (eds. J.E. McCosker, and M.D. Lagios). Occ. Pap. Cal. Acad. Sci. no., *134:* 56–67.

Worthington, J. (1906) The descriptive anatomy of the brain and cranial nerves of *Bdellastoma domberyi.* Quart. J. Micro. Sci., *49:* 137–181.

Wourms, J.P., J.W. Atz, and M.D. Stribling (1991) Viviparity and the maternal-embryonic relationship in the coelacanth, *Latimeria chalumnae.* Env. Biol. Fish., *32:* 225–248.

Subject Index

Octaval nerve
    ganglion *plate I*, 34
    rami 34, 35
Octavolateralis nerves,
    see Lateral line and Octaval
      nerves
Oculomotor nerve
    anastomosis 13, 18, 47
    ciliary ganglion cells *plate I*,
      plate II, 11, 19, 45–47, 60
    innervation
      eye 45–47, 60
      muscle *plate II*, 47
    peripheral course *plate II*, 9–13,
      19
    phylogeny 44–47
    ramules *plate II*, 9–13, 19
    structure 11, 13
Olfactory organ
    epithelial folds 6, 7, 18, 41, 42
    morphology 6–8, 18, 41, 42
    nerve
      fascicle bundles 6, 18
      lengths 6, 42, 43
      phylogeny 43, 44, 60
      tetrapod similarity 43
Optic nerve
    changes during development 43
    decussation 43, 45
    phylogeny 43–45
    plicateness 7, 10, 11, 43, 60
    structure 7, 11, 43

Phylogenetic comparisons 40–42,
    44, 59–61
Profundal nerve
    anastomosis, oculomotor nerve
      plate I, 18, 19
    course *plate I*, 7–10, 12, 17–19,
      21, 22
    function 22, 24
    ganglion *plate I*, 12, 17, 19, 20,
      48, 60
    phylogeny 44, 47, 48, 60
    ramules *plate I*, 7–10, 12, 17–19,
      21, 22, 48, 60
    rostral organ innervation 48

Rostral organ *plate I*, 7, 8
    embryology 54
    function 53
    innervation 19, 21, 22, 30–32,
      48, 53, 60

Spiracular chamber *plate II*, 12, 34,
    51, 54, 61

Terminal nerve 43
Trigeminal nerve
    anastomoses
      facial nerve *plate I*, 8, 27
      lateral line nerve 26, 49, 50
    course *plate I*, 7–10, 12, 14,
      24–26, 48
    ganglion *plate I*, 20, 21, 24–27,
      49
    organization 49, 55
    phylogeny 44, 47–50, 60
    ramules *plate I*, 7–10, 12, 25–27,
      49, 50, 60
Trochlear nerve
    muscle innervation *plate II*, 13,
      47
    peripheral course *plate II*, 10,
      12, 13
    phylogeny 44, 47

Vagal nerve
    composition 38
    course *plate I*, 38, 39
    ganglia *plate I*, 16, 23, 24, 38,
      57, 58, 61
    organization 38, 57, 58
    phylogeny 57, 58
    rami *plate I*, 10, 12, 14–16, 38,
      39, 57, 58, 61
    roots *plate I*, 38
Vomeronasal organ 43